PRAISE FOR *70 SECONDS:*

"I LOVE Dan's new book on leadership. I  ...ed many sermons on Joshua's character and ...ne to start teaching and preaching on this su... ...eat biblical depth to inspire. You will be blessed if you buy this book.

Al Robertson, Author, Speaker
and Star of A&E's Duck Dynasty

"In *70 Seconds*, Dan Holland takes a refreshing look at one of God's seminal lessons for life and leadership. In today's world we are often left wondering how to interpret the scriptures God has left for us. In this book Dan does an amazing job of showing us a modern-day biblical perspective that is not only highly applicable, but interesting and entertaining. I encourage you to read it and apply these principles to your life."

Nick Nanton, Esq., EMMY®
Award Winning Director/Producer;
Wall St. Journal Best-Selling Author

"Rediscover practical lessons from a favorite story of courage and faith . . . then prepare to unleash your leadership potential! Brilliant!"

Ruth T. Reyes, Ed.D.,
Professor of Music; Assistant Dean,
School of Communication
and Creative Arts

"Regardless of your current circumstances, *70 Seconds* will inspire you by revealing sound principles and practical actions you can take to improve your leadership abilities as a Christ follower. Dan Holland's book is readable, insightful and provocative for all aspiring leaders who are dissatisfied with the status quo and determined to improve their leadership skills and the lives of believers around them."

Bob Russell, Former Senior Minister,
Southeast Christian Church

"Dan Holland is a wise man. He's taken the wonderful biblical story of Joshua and the Hebrew children and brought to life the hidden, yet necessary, jewels of successful leadership. *70 Seconds* is a fast, easy, yet challenging read that makes sense of how to manage the call to leadership and be successful. It's a must read for all who would lead."

Rev. Alfred H. Ells, M.C.,
Leaders that Last Ministries

"This book will inspire you to search for your own gift of leadership as you see Joshua develop under God's guidance."

Lynn McMillon, Ph.D.,
Distinguished Professor of Bible,
Oklahoma Christian University

"Much of life is won or lost by how we think. In *70 Seconds* Dan Holland cracks open scripture, examines the life of Joshua, and explores the powerful connection between thought, action, and destiny."

Scot Longyear, Senior Pastor,
Maryland Community Church

"I've known Dan Holland for more than thirty years and this book is a beautiful watermark of his faith. It is an enlightening read that reminds you that God desperately desires to use you in EVERY chapter of your life. He skillfully communicates that trusting fully in God's love and promises are the keys to successfully getting through the adventures he calls you to. This book challenges you to walk bravely into the arena of your life and to listen carefully for what God is calling you to do!"

"Dan Holland has hit a home run with this book! It is encouraging and applies to us today as believers in Christ to have a heart like Joshua and apply the truths that I had never seen about him before. I hope you enjoy this book as much as I did and change some things on how you lead others. I know it has impacted me, and I will look at things differently now going forward in my life."

"Wow! Did I need this book! Dan Holland has done a masterful job in bringing us back to what really matters when our backs are up against the "walls" of life. FAITH!...not intellect.... not talent...not money....FAITH! Read this simple, yet powerful biblically based book that can change your perspective on how to handle anything the world throws at you. Remember, God says, 'I will never leave you!'"

"Monuments are God's idea. They mark moments that are critical to growing and changing and trusting God. In *70 Seconds*, Dan Holland highlights monuments that changed the course of history and can change your history as well!"

"I've held leadership positions in the corporate world for more than three decades. I've also had the chance to serve and lead in community-based organizations. *70 Seconds* addresses many of the issues that I've dealt with as a leader.

A successful leader must have strong core values that keep them focused on who they are. Holland's examples of how Joshua found success by following God's will reminds us of staying true to our core values and continuing to seek.

His Ten Leadership Highlights are on point. Anyone in a leadership position should read these and post them by their desk. I was particularly struck his your assessment that under Joshua, the Israelites discovered that it's on God's timetable, not ours.

I also took note of his chapters 'Dealing with Trouble' and 'Get Back Up.' From personal experience I believe that a successful life is built on years of overcoming failures. I believe we are judged not on what we have, but what we do with what we have.

Holland's study of Joshua reminds us to accept accountability (a rare trait in America these days) and get back on our feet after we fail.

He provides another treasure on the book with his 6 Steps to Regaining Confidence after Failure.

Finally, he makes the point that God's charge to Joshua can be read in *70 Seconds*. Too often we over think our charge when we should Keep It Simple."

Stan Knott, USA Pyramid Management

"Is your walk with Christ advancing or wandering (wondering)? Dan Holland has taken God's *70 Seconds* of instruction to Joshua (Joshua 1:1-9) and provided a frame work for anyone to quickly map out their life's path and Christian pace. Knowing your level of spiritual momentum and direction are the next steps in growing closer to your goals in faith."

Tom Jarzynka, Associate Certified Entomologist;
Senior Director of Pest Prevention
Quality Assurance | Massey Services, Inc.

"*70 seconds* is an example of Joshua developing and flexing his spiritual muscle in leading a stiff-necked people to the promised land. It's refreshing to know that even in our day today, following Joshua's example still works! The author knows this well...I watched him live it!"

Bob Beckler, Senior Pastor,
Central Community Church

"This book will serve as a resource guide for many leaders. Dan Holland teaches us through the life of Joshua that leadership matters on every level. Joshua used his experiences as a place of reference, but not as a place of residence. This resource will be a compass for many to navigate through the changing seasons of leadership."

David S. Jacques, Pastor of
The Kingdom Church

"In today's way of thinking, faith, love and contentment have disappeared because of a separation from God. In *70 Seconds,* Dan Holland gives a blue print for life, love and leadership. It doesn't matter how young or old you are, *70 Seconds* reminds us that there are hardships and missteps as seen through biblical history, but you can overcome by faith in Jesus. Dan conveys, in an incredible and understandable way, with God we can overcome and thrive."

Jim Morris, The Rookie

"In *70 Seconds* Dan Holland opens a door into the life and leadership of Joshua, exploring not only the fascinating history of God's very personal dealings with the Israelites after the wilderness wanderings, but also the driving forces that formed and sustained one of Israel's most versatile commanders. With clear insight and warm personal anecdotes, Holland illustrates the 'How To' of putting faith into action and claiming God's promises and rewards for God-given leadership at all levels. I heartily recommend this book to anyone wondering what God has in store for them, and how, exactly, to get started building a monument worthy life."

Melanie Hunter, Partner at
Hunter & Kalinke

"It is always a powerful and sacred 'moment' when God interrupts our wandering and directs us to a new and better future. You will have several 'moments' like this as you read *70 Seconds*...I did."

Jack Hilligoss, Lead Pastor, Highpoint Church;
Author of *Untouchables* and *Say What?*

"Dan Holland's book *70 Seconds* takes the complex issue of leadership faced by Joshua and puts it in context for today's leaders. He shows the reader how business and personal challenges can be overcome using the guiding principles of faith, obedience and courage that worked then and still work today. This is an essential read for those that want to be the leader that God designed them to be."

Beverly Stewardson, VP Human Capital at USMD Health System/
OptumCare, Southern Methodist University

"It is not just me? It is too easy to think I am the only one who is overwhelmed, overworked, and overburdened with life. In *70 Seconds*, Dan uses Joshua's life in a simple and understandable way to realize I am 'under-faithed.' The book's unique look at Joshua and God's charge reminds me that God is with me 'wherever I go.' If you ever wanted to get a handle on mixed up priorities – buy, rent, borrow.... Read *70 Seconds* by Dan Holland; you will be challenged to live in God's presence."

Jack Hightower, Managing Director
at Expense Reduction Analysts

"I've known Dan Holland as a tremendous preacher, teacher and wise friend for nearly thirty years. But my respect has increased even higher with *70 Seconds!* Although Dan's words are geared toward leaders, his insights will help anyone who needs inspiration to get unstuck or courage to overcome fear. I will tell everyone I know about this book."

Lorri Allen, Speaker; Radio &
TV Personality; Author of *It's All Good News!*

"In *70 Seconds*, Dan Holland illustrates through Joshua how God uses common people to accomplish amazing things...when we trust and obey Him with a faithful heart. *70 Seconds* will inspire you, that regardless of your age or position, God wants to work through you!"

Steve Stiger, President & CEO,
Good Life Broadcasting, Inc.

"*70 Seconds* is a fresh new perspective on leadership principles founded on solid Biblical truths. The concepts presented in the book are well organized, easy to read and understandable."

Steve Bush, Administrative Pastor,
Real Life Christian Church

"It is rare to find someone who excels in both leadership and Bible teaching, but Dan Holland shows us in *70 Seconds* that he is gifted in both and uniquely qualified to reveal the powerful insights on leadership hidden in this story.

I plan to buy several copies and share with my management team and my family."

David Hogan, Managing Director,
Ronald Blue & Co., CPAs and Consultants

"This book can't help but encourage your faith and challenge you to take your leadership to the next level. I have had the privilege to know Dan Holland and his family for more than twenty-five years. I have worked alongside him and experienced his leadership first hand. *70 Seconds* will renew your faith and strengthen your courage to lead with excellence!"

Jim Patterson, Vice President & COO,
ELEVATE Orlando

"In a time when leadership is the most needed comes a close examination of Joshua, God's servant, God's trusted—a picture of faith, execution and perseverance. Leadership is more than being in charge; it is a blind faith allowing God's power to enable you to lead people into a promised land and selling them a vision that we all can be leaders—in our jobs and the daily interactions with others. *70 Seconds* provides clear guidance we can utilize every day to implement His plan for us and 'be strong and courageous.'"

Kathleen Wall, Senior HIM Consultant,
Nuance Communications

"I'm impressed with the easy to read style and the message of *70 Seconds*. Every chapter is insightful and practical. This is a terrific book that readers can and will use to make monumental changes in their life."

Joe Sherwood, CWS Communities

"Absolutely critical truths for every season of life and leadership. This a great book. Part of my endorsement of this book is that I've watched Dan Holland live out the practical wisdom in these pages for nearly thirty years. *70 Seconds* isn't just a book with a few tips on living, it's a book that will actually help you build a successful life on the foundation of Jesus Christ."

Jamey Miller, Lead Pastor, Antioch Community Church;
President, Share Life Now International, serves on the
US Oversight Team for The Antioch Movement

"In *70 Seconds* Dan Holland challenges believers in God to do just that: BELIEVE in GOD – in his commands, in His promises, and in His Love. The results of which can be truly life changing."

Greg Lee, Actor, TV host
("Where in the World is Carmen Sandiego?"),
voice over artist (the voice of Mayor
White on ABC's "Doug"), Writer, Producer

"*70 Seconds* is a courageous call to Christian leadership. In *70 Seconds*, Dan helps the reader bridge the gap from Joshua's monumental task in history to a leader's challenges today. As a leader, your challenges are not Joshua's, but God's instruction to Joshua may be the exact word He wants you to hear and follow. Dan's thoughtful work is simultaneously convicting, constructive and compelling."

Greg Beauchamp,
Co-Pastor, Christ Church Irving

"I have often said that a well-placed question can change the direction of a person's life forever. In *70 Seconds*, Dan Holland walks through the kinds of questions that have the potential to disarm you and disrupt your life. But if you want to move past your past, or you want to avoid making the same mistakes as others, I recommend you think through some of the powerful questions that he poses in this thought-provoking book."

Rick Bezet, Lead Pastor of New Life Church;
Author of *Real Love in an Angry World* and
Be Real, Because Fake Is Exhausting

"When God places something in a person's heart, you know it. It's like a deposit that has been fashioned by God's wisdom over a long period of time until it is ready to bless His body. This book is one of those. It makes sense. It is practical, and it is well thought out. I liked it and gained a lot from simply doing my job."

Ellen M. King, Freelance Content Editor

"Dan not only brings Joshua's story to life, but brings it to your life! He gives you practical steps to take you from where you are to the promised life God designed!"

Matt Manzari, Burn Survivor /Speaker

"Don't let the title mislead you; it may have only taken 70 seconds for God to give these instructions to Joshua, but it will take you a lifetime to fully lean into living them out. I have known Dan in ministry for over 30 years and can tell you he not only teaches us what we need to know about fulfilling our leadership calling in this book, he also lived them for decades. Dan speaks from a personal knowledge of applying these principles in his life. As they have made him a great leader, they will do the same for you."

Greg Wiens, Chief Catalyst,
Healthy Growing Leaders

"I couldn't put it down. What a blessing it was to me! I realized right away that I have been WANDERING for the last couple of months! Reading *70 Seconds* has given me a newfound energy and dedication to staying faithful and making sure that I 'vote' every day. I am now thinking that maybe this season of my life is part of God's plan to give me rest and help me to really listen for His voice to determine what's next for me and to choose FAITH over fear!"

Joi Williams, former head coach,
UCF Women's Basketball;
former asst. coach,
WNBA San Antonio Stars

70
SECONDS

STOP WANDERING; START LIVING & LEADING!

- 7 core beliefs that will change the choices you make
- A new mindset you need to lead successfully
- How to handle adversity with faith not fear

DAN HOLLAND

70 Seconds: Stop Wandering; Start Living & Leading
by Dan Holland

Copyright © 2017 Dan Holland
All rights reserved

Published by HigherLife Development Services, Inc.
PO Box 623307
Oviedo, Florida 32762
(407) 563-4806
www.ahigherlife.com

ISBN 13: 978-0-9994156-2-7
ISBN 10: 099941562X

First Edition
13 14 15 16 17 —12 11 10 9 8 7 6 5
Printed in the United States of America

DEDICATION

To my dad, Don Holland. Your love for Jesus and teaching that faith will tell you what to do and love will tell you how inspires me everyday. I miss you.

To Micah and Ashley, my children, who never gave up on me over the years that I worked on researching and writing this material. I love you and am thankful to be your dad.

This book would not have been possible without the love and encouragement of my wife, Beth. Thank you for your support throughout the process of writing *70 Seconds*. While my love for you can be expressed in seconds, it is enough to fill the rest of our life together, to which I am looking forward. I love you.

ACKNOWLEDGEMENTS

This book project has had so many encouragers that it is impossible to make a complete list of thank yous. However, I do wish to thank:

Bob Russell, Kent Allen, Doug Kostowski, Greg Wiens, and Charles Wise. God used each of you to give me vital input at a time when I needed it most. You listened carefully and then spoke honestly and kindly to me. Thank you. Solomon was correct: "Though one may be overpowered, two can defend themselves. A cord of three strands is not quickly broken" (Ecc. 4:12). I hope every leader has people like you in their pit crew.

I am indebted to Melanie Hunter, who during the early stages of the manuscript brought vital perspective, biblical insight, and organization to the material.

Words cannot express my gratitude to Krista Petty for her professional advice and assistance in editing and collaboration on the original manuscript.

Val Hopkins and Jeff Raines who each played a significant role in helping to make this project become a reality because you encouraged me in many ways.

Bret Testerman and Carol Darling who gave significant feedback for the sermon series *The Monuments of Joshua: The Seven Most Important Stories of Your Life.*

I'll be forever grateful to David Welday and the Higher Life Publishing team who came together to make this book excellent: Laura Mathis for graciously guiding the process, Ellen M. King for her excellent editing and Larry J. Leech II for outstanding copyediting.

TABLE OF CONTENTS

INTRODUCTION

THE BOOK'S UNIQUE insights inspired by the *70 Seconds* of instruction God gave to Joshua make for an engaging read. Belief is where everything starts. This is a book about belief and the thoughts, actions, habits, and character that it takes to lead through the challenges of life. The message speaks to those who have been humbled by life's circumstances, had their faith tested through hardship, or are weary of wandering aimlessly through daily life. My hope is you will turn your faith loose in every area of your life. And also that your faith will shift from something that is simply available to you to a faith that beckons you into God's adventurous will for your life. This book offers hope and a way through a world that is looking for something solid, unchanging, and reliable on which to anchor their beliefs. Joshua stayed the course through his challenges, and you can too!

70 SECONDS!

SEVENTY SECONDS IS all it took for God to tell Joshua everything he needed to know to successfully lead His people. How could that be? Since God created this whole thing called life, odds are high that He knows how it works. What struck me about God's instructions is not only what He said, but also what He *didn't* say. It was obvious that God's people would face fierce armies, yet not a word was given about military strategy, or specifics about the terrain or the enemy.

Joshua's success, and the success of God's people, was more of a matter of faithfulness to God than skill, strategy, and intelligence. Please don't misunderstand me. I am not saying that it doesn't matter if a person is incompetent, disorganized, and ignorant. I am reminding you that faith is the key ingredient. Don't fall into the trap of believing that if you could just sharpen your skill, revamp your strategy, and become shrewder, then every-

> FAITH IS THE KEY INGREDIENT. DON'T FALL INTO THE TRAP OF BELIEVING THAT IF YOU COULD JUST SHARPEN YOUR SKILL, REVAMP YOUR STRATEGY, AND BECOME SHREWDER, THEN EVERYTHING WILL BE BETTER.

thing will be better. Leaders must rise above the circumstances in which they find themselves, while continuing to lead within the context of those circumstances. God is able to use the circumstances that you are currently in to build you into the man or woman that He has created you to be. Change your mindset to fully embrace where God has you, and trust Him. Let faith lead you rather than fears drive you. Biblically, God always measures success in terms of faithfulness rather than any other category on the balance sheet. Imagine, seventy seconds to the life God desires for you—a life built on faith. Here's what happened:

> *"After the death of Moses the servant of the Lord, the Lord said to Joshua son of Nun, Moses' aide: "Moses my servant is*

dead. Now then, you and all these people, get ready to cross the Jordan River into the land I am about to give to them—to the Israelites. I will give you every place where you set your foot, as I promised Moses. Your territory will extend from the desert to Lebanon, and from the great river, the Euphrates—all the Hittite country—to the Mediterranean Sea on the west. No one will be able to stand against you all the days of your life. As I was with Moses, so I will be with you; I will never leave you nor forsake you. Be strong and courageous, because you will lead these people to inherit the land I swore to their ancestors to give them. Be strong and very courageous. Be careful to obey all the law my servant Moses gave you; do not turn from it to the right or to the left, that you may be successful wherever you go. Keep this Book of the Law always on your lips; meditate on it day and night, so that you may be careful to do everything written in it. Then you will be prosperous and successful. Have I not commanded you? Be strong and courageous. Do not be afraid; do not be discouraged, for the Lord your God will be with you wherever you go" (Joshua 1:1-9).

You can read that in seventy seconds. Everything Joshua needed to hear was in these powerful words spoken by the Lord in just over a minute. This book will explore the ideas found in this passage and empower you to apply these truths to your life as well.

It only takes *70 Seconds*!

JOSHUA, THE MONUMENT BUILDER

You are a leader.

You probably wouldn't have picked up this book if you weren't already a leader or preparing to be one. Your leadership might be in your home, at your work, in your community, or within your church. What if you could get your hands on a foolproof map that would take you to a successful life of leadership in all those places? Would you take the time to *unfold* it? What if you could glean insight from a seasoned mentor, coaching you towards success? This book is for people who want to thrive; and for whatever reason, might feel stuck.

I believe one of the most powerful books on Christian leadership is found in the Bible: the book of Joshua. *70 Seconds* was written to guide you through that book. Many think Joshua is the record of a conquest, but I see it is much more than that. It is a map to the beliefs, thoughts, actions, habits, and character that it takes to lead ourselves and others into God's rest and the life He has promised. In these pages, I hope you will unfold God's plan for creating steadfast leaders, worthy of building monuments that point to Him. Joshua's life can mentor you; and we know we can trust him because we have his story right in front of us. He wasn't a perfect man, but he stayed the course.

I first encountered the book of Joshua during a season of forced rest. Twenty-three years ago, just after my son was born and I was in the throes of a crazy ministry schedule, I developed a cough. It was irritating but I didn't have time to stop and tend to it. Finally, the cough got annoying enough that I went to a doctor. She ran some tests. I had a severe case of mononucleosis.

"The kissing disease?" I asked her.

"Yes, and you can go home and go to bed. If you go back to work, I'm going to put you in the hospital," she said.

I laughed.

She didn't.

And so began my four weeks of forced rest. During my time in bed, I read Joshua. I examined these monuments and the moments leading up to them. God was pointing to some important things. The very common Hebrew word *yād*, which means hand, in a few instances meant *monument*, a reflection of the hand's function of pointing.[1] These monuments were (and are) intended to remind God's people of lessons learned in the past, but in such a way that recalling the event might inform their current beliefs, thoughts, and actions. God wanted His people to live fully in the present while being informed by His actions in the past. The hope was that their faith would be strengthened so they could boldly face their daily challenges, struggles, and problems.

I became infatuated with this story and of course, being a preacher, I had to teach it. I developed a series. Since that time, I have preached about Joshua many times, in many settings. Each time, more is revealed. Like our mentor, Joshua, I have experienced many ups and downs in life and leadership. I believe I've matured a bit since that first in-depth reading of the book. God has used the story of Joshua to mentor and coach me through both joyous and tough seasons in life and ministry, and I'd like to introduce you to him.

Meet Joshua: God's Chosen Monument Builder

We are first introduced to Joshua as the military field commander under Moses shortly after the Israelites exodus from Egypt. Joshua turned out to be a great military leader who confidently led Israel to conquer Canaan after the death of Moses. However, as is usually the case, there is more to the story. His physical strength and might were not what conquered Canaan, as some might expect. Joshua was ninety years old when he led Israel into Canaan, so I don't imagine him as one of those warriors out there slinging a sword in battle.

While Joshua's life may look somewhat glamorous at first glance, a deeper look shows his life had not been an easy one. Yes, his remarkable life was filled with excitement, variety, success, and honor. But he also experienced hardship, suffering, failure, and loss. He experienced the bitter realities of slavery in Egypt until he was fifty. He got a front row seat to the supernatural plagues as God prepared to deliver His people from the Egyptians. He experienced walking on dry ground through the Red Sea as walls of water stood at attention to his left and right. After such an awesome experience, it only got better as he was one of the twelve men chosen to investigate Canaan. His faith in God won out over the giants he and Caleb saw while spying out the Promised Land for Moses.

Though Joshua and Caleb were unsuccessful in counteracting the unbelieving, negative, pessimistic attitudes of the other ten spies, God rewarded their courage and faith by promising them entrance into the Promised Land. However, before that promise could be fulfilled they had to first spend forty years in the wilderness, thanks to their unbelieving friends. Like Joshua, leadership is marked by peaks and valleys, but as we will see, *successful* leadership is marked by faithfulness.

Enter the Promised Life

Have you ever had your dreams dashed by the doubts and fears of others? Joshua did, yet even this monumental setback did not turn him bitter or cynical. Both he and his sidekick, Caleb, kept their faith in God rather than circumstances and kept their minds fixed on God's promise. Joshua's life beautifully parallels this verse in the New Testament:

> *"So we fix our eyes not on what is seen, but on what is unseen,*
> *since what is seen is temporary, but what is unseen is eternal"*
> (2 Corinthians 4:18).

The Christian experience of living in Christ parallels the experiences of God's Old Testament people entering Canaan. As they had a Promised Land, we have a promised life, both in the present and the future. Entering the historic Promised Land was the fulfillment of the ancient pledge God made to

Israel's ancestors: Abraham, Isaac and Jacob. Entering the promised life is the fulfillment of God's new covenant to us through Jesus Christ.

God's desire for His people, both then and now, is to be freed from oppression and from the mindset that keeps us living that way. Jesus said, *"I came that they might have life and have it abundantly"* (John 10:10b, ESV). Along our journey in Joshua, I hope you will be encouraged to step into your promised life.

What Happened Here? And Other Powerful Questions

The story of Joshua is easy to follow because it has a clear beginning, middle, and ending, and is marked by seven specific monuments during the time of the conquest. Like bookmarks in the pages of history, the monuments of Joshua reminded God's people of important choices. Each monument was—and still is—intended to spark the memory of what happened at that place, to remind God's people of His faithfulness, and how their choices to live by faith and obedience influenced God's involvement in their lives. God even instructed that the history and lessons be taught to future generations for their benefit. That includes you and me.

> ALL MONUMENTS CAUSE US TO ASK: "WHAT HAPPENED HERE?" THAT IS A POWERFUL QUESTION ABOUT THE PAST THAT CAN INFLUENCE THE WAY WE SEE THE FUTURE.

A monument or memorial can mark a victory, like the Wright Brothers National Memorial in Kill Devils Hill, North Carolina, marking man's first flight, or sorrow and defeat like the Vietnam Veterans Memorial in Washington D.C. All monuments cause us to ask: "What happened here?" That is a powerful question about the past that can influence the way we see the future. On our journey through Joshua, we will tackle some other powerful questions. Powerful questions can potentially disrupt your world because they cause your thoughts to travel new paths.

Although disruptive, these monumental questions can help you gain clarity about your life and break free of the gravitational pull of the status quo, charting a course toward greater meaning, joy, and impact instead. Some of the questions we will explore are:

- How can I stop wandering and prepare to advance?
- What are God's promises to me?
- How can I develop faith instead of fear in unfamiliar territory?
- Will I be able to handle trouble when it comes my way?
- Do I have what it takes to persevere during setbacks (because doubt and disappointments are part of the promised life too)?
- How can I pace myself and listen to God?
- How can I make effective use of failure?
- What does it take to lead towards unity and harmony?
- How will I finish strong and prepare the next leaders?

Measurable Results

One of the most difficult business models to dismantle is one that *appears* to be working. Appearances can be deceiving. The same is true as we travel through life. Often, until we are sufficiently wounded, the desire and motivation to live monumentally remains elusive. Things may *appear* to be working, but internally we aren't so sure.

Most successful leaders take time at the end of the year to assess their results. They don't just recount stories of how their business served people, or anecdotes of how their profits grew. They look at metrics— real measurable results. When I ask business owners if their company was firing on all eight cylinders, I also ask them to tell me how they would know that. When I do, they have an immediate answer. But when I ask about their personal life, seldom do they have metrics for their personal lives.

> WHEN I ASK ABOUT THEIR PERSONAL LIFE, SELDOM DO THEY HAVE METRICS FOR THEIR PERSONAL LIVES.

Imagine that it's New Year's Eve. Midnight has come and gone, and everyone in your house has gone to bed. You sit by the fire alone with God, looking back over the year. After making some critical decisions, you have been living with fresh clarity for the entire year, and you sense you are operating in the sweet spot of your unique contribution. For some of you that will be in a marketplace role, for others in a church role, or possibly in your family or community. Most likely, it will be a blend of all those things. Whatever you are doing, you are certain it's your calling.

As you sit reflecting, you realize at the deepest part of your being that you are living the perfect life—the promised life. How will you know you are living the perfect life? What will be the metrics by which you come to that conclusion? Notice that I am not asking you what you would be doing. This is an even deeper question. How did you get there?

> THE MONUMENTS OF JOSHUA CAN BE THE BIBLICAL, PRACTICAL, AND SIGNIFICANT MEASURABLE METRICS FOR YOUR LIFE.

The more clearly you can answer this question, the easier it will be to build a strategy to get there. The monuments of Joshua can help you define those metrics. The monuments of Joshua can be the biblical, practical, and significant measurable metrics for your life. Success, as seen in Joshua, are not your typical metrics, but they are vital. On a scale of 1-10, get out your journal and rate how you are growing in these areas:

- I am taking risks to follow God, even going into unfamiliar territory.
- I am learning from the past, not running from it; and I am letting the past inform my future, not hold me back.
- I am dealing with troublesome people and difficult circumstances instead of avoiding them.
- I am developing perseverance.
- I am quick to obey God's instruction and have found a rhythm to life which keeps me in spiritual alignment.

- I am trustworthy, accepting responsibility swiftly.
- I am an active peacemaker, not divisive and at the same time, not passive.
- I am secure in who I am, what I stand for, and I am investing in others.

These are the metrics we see in the book of Joshua. There may be some areas in which you already excel, but I'm guessing that, like me, there is great opportunity for growth.

You Can Do This. Yes, YOU!

Maybe you are well on the way to your pinnacle of successful leadership, and are just interested in a few pointers—signs to show you how to get around barriers to the promised life. Or, like many, you are coasting along, wondering if something is missing. Perhaps you are in a valley of defeat, at a dead end, or desperately hoping to find a way to avoid abysmal failure, or at least save some face. Do you think it is too late to find the abundant, promised life? It's never too late to believe. Belief is the starting place for changing the trajectory of your life.

Joshua was a fifty-year-old slave named Hoshea when Moses showed up to demand that Pharaoh release the Hebrews, and a ninety-year-old when he was called to lead the nation of Israel after Moses's death. And let's not forget that Moses was an eighty-year-old fugitive convict-turned-shepherd when God called him to be His emissary. So here we have as our two fearless leaders: Joshua, a fifty-year-old slave, and Moses, an eighty-year-old fugitive. The point is that as long as you are breathing, it's never too late. You may not be up in years, but even as a young leader you may have had leadership curveballs thrown at you that make you feel weathered and worn. You can rise above obstacles and trade fear for new dreams. Those you lead will take notice of your faith and perseverance.

Not only were these leaders aging, Joshua's position as the designated leader began at the precarious time when the generation that had known the horribly oppressive slavery in Egypt had all died. Moses, their deliverer, was also dead. The saying, "You've got some big shoes to fill" is true in this case. Maybe you are feeling inadequate because, like Joshua, you have some big shoes to fill.

Despite their difficult circumstances, God used both Moses and Joshua to teach people about Him, and train them in the abundant life He intended them to have. Those lessons can lead you to the promised life too.

Your *Source* Matters More than Your *Size*

Joshua was a man of faith whether circumstances were horrific or terrific. Why? His faith was in God rather than in actual outcomes. The *direction* of your faith has a lot more to do with its impact on your life than the *size* of it. Joshua's faith, big or small, found its source in God. It may be that because of his faith he was chosen for important assignments. In the Sinai Peninsula, it was Joshua who led the troops of Israel to victory over the Amalekites (See Exodus 17:8-13). He was the only person allowed to accompany Moses up the mountain when the tablets of the Law were received (See Exodus 24:13-14). And it was he who stood watch at the temporary tent of meeting Moses set up before the tabernacle was erected (See Exodus 33:11).

Faith Is a Choice

How did Joshua respond to the opportunities and challenges of life? The answer to that question is the heartbeat of Joshua's decision-making process. His response to fifty years as a slave in Egypt was to wait on God. His chosen response to the giants and challenges in the Promised Land was to depend on God. And his response to forty years in the wilderness was to follow and, again, wait on God. Just as he did not choose bitterness or cynicism from his experiences, neither did he become prideful or overconfident when his circumstances dramatically improved. Maybe this is why he is remembered for his deep trust in God, as *"...a man in whom is the spirit of leadership..."* (Num. 27:18).

You might be familiar with the two verses that bookend Joshua's story. This is what God said at the beginning of his official role as leader:

> *"Have I not commanded you? Be strong and courageous. Do not be afraid; do not be discouraged, for the Lord your God will be with you wherever you go"* (Joshua 1:9).

This was his assertion of faith after seven years of war:

> *"But as for me and my household, we will serve the Lord"* (Joshua 24:15b).

Do you have the faith necessary to assure the people who follow you that the Lord is with them?

Yes, I think you do. The real question is whether the reader has that same faith.

Will you have that same unwavering and humble faith after years of agonizing defeat, unexpected setbacks, failed attempts, as well as thrilling victories?

Yes, I think you will. Journey through Joshua with me and discover how.

Chapter 1

STOP WANDERING. ADVANCE.

Life has no remote...get up and change it yourself!

The Stuck-But-Predictable Life

FOR THE FIRST fifty years of Joshua's life, one day looked very much like the previous one. Life became increasingly difficult as Pharaoh leaned into the Hebrew people. Joshua and the entire Hebrew nation had shelter, clothes, and food, but it was a hard life. Getting out of Egypt would prove to be more challenging than I'm sure any of them could ever have imagined. The new Pharaoh pressed God's people down so far that they cried out to God to save them. And He heard them.

God sent Moses to deliver them. On the road leading from the stuck-but-predictable life to the promised life, things happened. As soon as the Israelites left Egypt, Pharaoh regretted letting them go. He sent his powerful, well-trained and heavily armed Egyptian army to bring them back. As the mighty Egyptian army approached from the west, Israel was facing the Red Sea in the east. They were in a pickle. To say they had doubts would be an understatement of mammoth proportions. "Were there not enough graves in Egypt?" the people complained to Moses, who, in turn, cried out to God and He delivered His people in a dramatic fashion, straight through the Red Sea into the promised life. Right? Not exactly. They wandered first.

And Joshua, son of Nun, was right there in the middle of it all. He was there in the enslavement, the deliverance, and the miraculous escape. He was watching, waiting, and following, long before he was called to lead the people into the Promised Land.

Why Did They Wander? Why Do We Wander?

As we will see, the reason the Israelites wandered, and why we wander, too, is simple. A quick summary of the story can be found in Hebrews 3 and 4.

> *"So we see that they were not able to enter, because of their unbelief"* (Hebrews 3:19).

And just a few verses later:

> *"...but the message they heard was of no value to them, because they did not share the faith of those who obeyed"* (Hebrews 4:2).

They knew the truth and they knew God's promise, but they did not combine the information they had with faith. You can have every ingredient but one and if you leave that one ingredient out, what you are baking will not turn out well.

If we will take what we know and put faith in it, it's amazing what happens in life, as we will see from Joshua's example. Unfortunately, we tend to lose our focus, or rather, we focus on the wrong things.

Ten Believed They Couldn't, So They Didn't

As they camped on the banks of the Jordan River before the Israelites entered the Promised Land, Moses sent twelve men to check out the land God promised to them—Canaan. It was described as a land flowing with milk and honey. This is where we first see Joshua and his buddy, Caleb together. They were two of the twelve chosen spies.[2]

Upon the spies' return to the Israelite camp, they agreed the land was more amazing and even better than they had anticipated. All twelve men also agreed that those living in the land were large. "Giants" was how they described the men,

16

living inside walled cities that were to become the homes of this freshly delivered nation of people. This is the only thing all twelve spies agreed on. Then, the spies part company. Ten spies said that living in the land wasn't possible because there were too many insurmountable obstacles. *"We seemed like grasshoppers in our own eyes, and we looked the same to them,"* reported the ten spies (Num. 13:33b). Even though God promised the land, it didn't appear doable. It wasn't practical. Feeling stuck again, God's people began to cry and shout.

Like far too many of us, they wanted something more in life but didn't want to put forth the effort to get it. The ten spies convinced the rest of the group that moving forward would be disastrous, and the people believed them instead of the promises of God. Why had they left their lives in Egypt? Sometimes the grass looks greener in the past when, in reality, it's not. The people longed to go back to Egypt and be enslaved. They knew what to expect there.

Have you ever found yourself in a predicament of a gigantic proportion and were willing to trade the promised life for the predictable past?

My Stuck-But-Predictable Life

Things had been going well in ministry until there was a shift in some leadership around me. I found myself in submission to some people I perceived as stubborn, and I wasn't able to communicate with them well. We were not on the same page. It was a frustrating situation for a number of years. I sought out mentors to help me—some of the best men and women Christian leaders I knew—hoping one of them would say a magic word that would change my situation. They gave me a lot of good advice and spiritual support. I knew, and they confirmed, that I was right in the situation. But "being right" didn't change the people around me, nor did it alleviate the suffering that came with these difficult relationships. No matter what I tried, I couldn't seem to make a dent in the prevailing leadership's mindset.

I was rehearsing the story of my circumstances yet again to one of my mentors. Things were not changing, people were stubbornly resisting a new way of thinking. They were not accepting help from myself or others, and protecting what they had instead. My situation was, indeed, sad. My mentor had heard it all before. At one point, I could tell that over the phone from a thousand miles away, he had just stopped listening. I stopped talking and politely hung up the phone.

Then it happened again. This time, I was talking with my wife, Beth. I was driving and she was in the passenger seat when I started rehearsing my frustration about work-related stuff. Then came the moment when I realized she had stopped listening too. Again, I stopped talking. After a moment of silence, Beth said, "I'm sorry. Go ahead with your story." I told her I didn't need to finish my story. The silence from both my mentor and my wife told me all I needed to know: Nobody could fix this for me. No one would come to rescue me. I was stuck. Things weren't what they used to be and were not what God intended for my life—my promised life. I realized that the problem had less to do with the other people and more to do with my choice to focus on the problems rather than God. I only saw the giants.

> I REALIZED THAT THE PROBLEM HAD LESS TO DO WITH THE OTHER PEOPLE AND MORE TO DO WITH MY CHOICE TO FOCUS ON THE PROBLEMS RATHER THAN GOD.

What's more, even if they could have fixed the situation, they shouldn't have. Fixing the situation for me would have enabled me to continue my search for others to fix things for me. My growth as a leader would have been stunted. The maturing process that God was working would have been interrupted. That one simple thought that "no one could fix my problems" shut me up, and caused me to wonder, "So what is my next step?" There were several options to remedy the situation. Each came with consequences...if only I could see what to do.

Two Saw the Promised Life

While ten spies saw obstacles, two saw opportunity. Joshua and Caleb acknowledged the challenge that lay ahead. The giants were real and big, but they knew God was also real, and that He was bigger than any of the challenges they might face. They said the people could move into the Promised Land, and that they absolutely should. What did they see that the other spies didn't? These two men saw God was on their side. They didn't ignore the enormity of the obstacles. They believed: "We can if God says we can!" And even beyond that, it's as if Caleb and Joshua were saying: "We will if God says we will!" They put the problem in proper perspective.

> LIVING IN OBEDIENCE TO GOD BY FAITH DOES NOT MEAN YOU IGNORE REALITY; RATHER LIVING IN OBEDIENCE AND BY FAITH IS LETTING REALITY BE DEFINED BY GOD.

Is there a problem in your life that needs to be placed in the proper perspective—to be seen through a lens of faith? Living in obedience to God by faith does not mean you ignore reality; rather living in obedience and by faith is letting reality be defined by God. Joshua and Caleb believed God would give them success because He had brought them this far. They believed God would lead them all the way.

> *"We should go up and take possession of the land, for we can certainly do it,"* Caleb told the people (Numbers 13:30b).

Herein lies the difference between wandering and advancing. One storyline has the majority of people confused, angry, disappointed, and wondering what will happen. That's always the story of a person's life whenever he or she loses sight of what God can do, and chooses to focus only on what they can do themselves. Whenever you choose to compare the size of your problem to your own personal abilities and resources, instead of comparing the size of the problem to the size of God's power and resources, you remain in a stuck-but-safe life. The

Israelites weren't where they used to be and they weren't where they intended to be; they were in-between.

Where are you?

Despite their personal circumstances or the attitudes of the people, Joshua and Caleb lived according to their convictions. Because they did, God did allow them, and only them and their descendants, to experience the promised life. Joshua spent fifty years in the stuck-but-predictable life and forty years in the in-between life, but the reward was that he got to live the last twenty years in the promised life when he entered the Promised Land. Joshua was always moving toward the promised life because he chose to focus on what God could do.

The Choice

Notice I said "Joshua chose." Realizing that I had the ability to choose was what changed my situation. I could change my situation, as well as my thoughts and feelings surrounding it. Rather than feeling hopeless, I now felt empowered. I could fix it. Why had I not seen it until now? Maybe you've wondered the same thing with a situation you found yourself in? Why had I not made decisions that were within my power to make, rather than talking about the ones that weren't? Maybe I had been blinded by my own warped sense of submission to misplaced leaders as somehow being God's will? It truly was a broken leadership group. The fact of the matter was that the situation was about me exerting my will with an unhealthy sense of protecting myself. My choices were having the opposite effect of what I desired.

Submission and choice do not live in separate zip codes; they are not mutually exclusive. After all, submission is a choice, but submission to God must come first. In a split second of silence from my mentor and my wife, I knew that by the grace of God and in His grace I could choose something else. I had the ability to think differently, believe deeply and live intentionally, and I knew that I would.

I still had unanswered questions running through my mind. How will this decision impact my family? How will this affect my reputation?

Whatever was not in my power to control I decided to willingly, gladly, and thankfully accept as the will of God, and desire that His strength would be made perfect in weakness, as Paul writes in 2 Corinthians 12:9. I figured if God did it for Paul, He could, and probably would, do the same for me. I also knew this meant I would have to accept hardship as divine discipline and I would stop any self-induced hardship. *Life is difficult enough without bringing hardship on myself,* I thought.

A New Trajectory

That simple realization—that I could choose—changed the trajectory of my life. Nothing outside of me had changed. Nothing external had changed, yet. The people around me had not changed. Yet this realization of choice ignited a new fire within me. A light switch in me was turned on and electricity flowed. It was not that I suddenly thought so much more of myself. I stopped thinking so little of

> I DID NOT HAVE A RENEWED FAITH IN MYSELF OR MY ABILITIES; I HAD A RENEWED FAITH IN GOD AND WHAT HE COULD DO.

myself. With a renewed focus on God, I could stop thinking of myself as small, insignificant, and helpless, and start thinking about myself in a proper perspective. I am a child of God and should live and act according to His power, not mine.

It also wasn't that I thought I would change everything, I *stopped* trying to change everything and everyone else. I stopped waiting for someone to rescue me. I did not have a renewed faith in myself or my abilities; I had a renewed faith in God and what He could do. I got serious about what God wanted more than what I wanted. I was thirsty, wanting what God wanted. He became my *why.* Pleasing Him became priority Number One in everything, everywhere, at all times. If I would fear God more than I feared any man, situation, or even failure, He would do what only He can do.

I find it most interesting that God has given humans the ability to choose. Even when it seems that all ability to choose has been removed, it remains that

I can choose my response. We can choose what to think, how to act, and which attitudes we will nurture. The God-given ability to choose must be given away; it cannot be taken. It must be relinquished of our own free will. In my situation, as my mindset changed so did my speech. As I said earlier, I stopped repeating the story. This was a new chapter! My words changed from, "Wouldn't it be nice if I had that kind of faith" to "I can do that!"

The Power of Mindset

The linchpin in my situation, and in Joshua and Caleb's, was realizing the power of *mindset*. The English Oxford Dictionary defines *mindset* as "the established set of attitudes held by someone."[3] To me, the sum of a person's mindset comes from a person's beliefs, and those beliefs determine our thoughts. Your thoughts are like the settings on a thermostat because they act as unequivocal set points—the temperature at which the switch is activated. If temperature is below the set point, the heater is on and the temperature rises. When the rising temperature passes the set point, the thermostat switches the heater off and the temperature falls passively.[4]

> EVEN WHEN OTHERS ARE UNRELIABLE, UNTRUSTWORTHY OR UNFAITHFUL, WE ARE CALLED TO BE RELIABLE, CREDIBLE, TRUSTWORTHY, STEADFAST, AND IN A WORD, FAITHFUL.

The Christian is asked to be a *thermostat*, not a *thermometer*. We are to set the temperature, not report the temperature. Even when others are unreliable, untrustworthy or unfaithful, we are called to be reliable, credible, trustworthy, steadfast, and in a word, faithful. Why? Because God is faithful to His promise, even when we are not.

Eventually, the temperature falls below the set point and the cycle repeats. What is your setting? Is your mind set to please God or yourself? Who is Lord and Master? The Bible teaches us to take care what we are thinking, since it might, in fact, be a self-fulfilling prophecy. Our direction in life springs from our hearts, so we need to govern our hearts and minds continually. This principle is most clearly stated in Proverbs 4:23:

> *"Keep your heart with all vigilance, for from it flow the springs of life"* (ESV).

> *"Guard your heart above all else, for it determines the course of your life"* (NLT).

What you feel and think in your heart is who you truly are. The heart is like a mirror. You are not what you see when you look at yourself from the outside; what you truly are is seen from the inside. You are not who others think you are, but rather who *you* think you are. Reset your heart as you would a thermostat.

You likely have heard Solomon quoted in this: that what you think of yourself is a self-fulfilling prophecy. I have often heard this in regard to man: *"For as he thinketh in his heart, so is he"* (Prov. 23:7, KJV). Yet what is the true context of that verse? Look at the interesting rendering of this verse in the *New International Version*: *"Do not eat the food of a begrudging host, do not crave his delicacies; for he is the kind of person who is always thinking about the cost.*

> YOU ARE NOT WHAT YOU SEE WHEN YOU LOOK AT YOURSELF FROM THE OUTSIDE; WHAT YOU TRULY ARE IS SEEN FROM THE INSIDE.

'Eat and drink,' he says to you, but his heart is not with you" (Prov. 23:6-7).

The way the man thinks has everything to do with the meal. He says and puts forth one idea, but in his heart he is complaining about the cost of the meal. He wants to appear generous to others, but in reality, he is stingy. His heart measures him. His heart is not with you as it appears to be. His heart is somewhere else. God must be the Lord and Master of our hearts, so we bring forth His fruit and accomplish His deeds.

Your mindset is the beginning point for this new life.

We read about Caleb's set point later in Joshua's story.

> Caleb said to Joshua, *"I was forty years old when Moses the servant of the Lord sent me from Kadesh Barnea to explore the land. And I brought him back a report according to my convictions, but my fellow Israelites who went up with me made the hearts of the people melt in fear. I, however, followed the Lord my God wholeheartedly"* (Joshua 14:7-8).

Arriving at a New Mindset

What are your convictions? The answer to this question is critical. This is the hard work you must do to arrive at a new mindset. A new mindset leads to a new life because thoughts lead to actions and habits, which determine our character and destiny. You will hear me say that *a lot.* The in-between life is filled with wandering—always moving but never arriving. It's a life filled with complaining, fear, grumbling or regret.

A NEW MINDSET LEADS TO A NEW LIFE BECAUSE THOUGHTS LEAD TO ACTIONS AND HABITS, WHICH DETERMINE OUR CHARACTER AND DESTINY.

That pretty well sums up the wilderness wandering for the Israelites, and it sums up my inner life in the time leading up to my big insight: "Dan, no one can fix this for you, but you can."

Attitudes can be indicators telling us whether we are living the in-between, wandering life, or the promised life. People who find themselves wandering have a mindset that is seldom settled and lacks direction and focus. This is why I call it the in-between or wandering life. People in a state of wandering also find themselves blaming and complaining.

The Israelites were free, but still had the mindset and attitudes of slaves. Similarly, I felt like a slave in my circumstances and complained to my mentors and wife about it. The wilderness was intended to be a place in which God's people were humbled and learned who they were and who God was.

24

Time to Set the Thermostat

How do you set your thermostat as Joshua did? What convictions will you position your mind so that in *any* situation, you are prepared to advance into the promised life? Let's explore some of Joshua's set points.

Setting 1: Believe God

I'm not sure when Joshua first learned about the promise made to Abram and later to Joseph, but from the first time we are introduced to him, he already had strong conviction that God could and would make good on His promise, someway, somehow.

Joshua believed God would bring His promise to fulfillment, even if he didn't know how it would be accomplished. I like that. It's tangible. It's real. Joshua believed God and so can I. I've had a long relationship with the Lord, but the day of my awakening it seemed like my faith got a shot of adrenaline that has never relented. So what are the promises of God we can use as our anchor? We will look at those specifically in the next chapter.

Joshua's name doesn't appear among the great people listed in the Hebrews 11, but it didn't have to be. The point wasn't that Joshua was great; it was that God is great. Joshua's faith was great not because of its size, but because of its focus—

> I HAD TO BELIEVE GOD, CONTROL MY MIND, THINK NEW THOUGHTS AND TRUST THAT HE WOULD GIVE ME WHAT I NEEDED, WHEN I NEEDED IT, AND PROBABLY NOT BEFORE.

on God. The story of Joshua reminds us that God is faithful to His promises. It highlights the possibility that if Joshua could believe God than so can we. It should make you say, "I can do that!"

I had to believe God, control my mind, think new thoughts and trust that he would give me what I needed, when I needed it, and probably not before. I was okay with accepting God's timing. I stopped talking about the past and retelling the story of who had done what, or said what. I stopped being angry with circumstances and people. I wanted a new chapter, so I turned the page. Have you ever tried driving forward while looking in the rearview mirror? It usually doesn't work out. Joshua and Caleb's mindset focused on the future, while they lived fully engaged in the present. This mindset feels empowered to choose and would rather focus on the truth about both others and ourselves. This mindset feels hopeful, free, and God-directed. This mindset understands and accepts its place and above all, trusts God. That is why I refer to it as the promised life.

More importantly, in my situation I had a renewed sense that what would please God most was if I trusted Him. That's when I officially became a seasoned optimist. I had to believe that God exists and that He would reward me if I diligently sought Him.

"And without faith it is impossible to please God, because anyone who comes to him must believe that he exists and that he rewards those who earnestly seek him" (Hebrews 11:6).

That's what I admire about Joshua. He trusted God regardless of what was happening around him. His circumstances didn't dictate his faith. His faith determined his response to his circumstances. Joshua's mindset determined the direction and purpose of his life, because it informed the choices he made. He believed God whether he was being oppressed in Egypt, humbled in the wilderness, or fighting in Canaan. Joshua constantly asked, "What does the Lord want *from* me? What does He want *for* me?"

There is a tendency to think if you can get to a certain place that everything will be easier. In my circumstance, I thought if I could just get the leaders to change or agree to my point of view, things would get better. Worse than that, there were moments when I would daydream, "If I could only get to the right church, or work with so and so instead..." Usually this kind of daydreaming is not helpful and serves only as an escape from dealing with reality and making the best of where you are. Perfect scenarios rarely happen. This kind of daydreaming can be dangerous because the situations we imagine are flawless, because they are not real.

The Israelites, too, were waiting for a flawless, perfect scenario before advancing. They didn't want to fight for their freedom. Yet, to live where God wanted them to live that's exactly what they needed to do. We don't often like to fight for what we want either. That brings us into the next three settings necessary to enter the promised life.

The "We Can" Mindset

When the twelve spies reported back to Moses and Aaron, the people heard only "we can't" instead of Joshua and Caleb's report that "with God, we can!" The dissention between the people and Joshua, Caleb, Moses, and Aaron got so heated, that at one point, the people wanted to stone their leaders. God was prepared to strike the people down with a plague when Moses again delivered the people by pleading with the Lord to spare them and show His glory and grace.

This began the forty long years of waiting to enter (one year for each of the forty days the spies explored the Promised Land). The mindset of slavery was so pervasive that it took forty years to get it out of them! God was angry, yet in this discipline He was also a loving Father. He knew His people were not ready to enter the Promised Land, for the simple reason they did not fully trust Him. In this time of waiting, God prepared the people by establishing offerings, the duties of the priests and Levites, and more. All He taught them in the wilderness encouraged them to focus their eyes on Him and His plan for them. He was growing and developing a whole new generation to step into the Promised Land while preparing Joshua to lead them.

God was disciplining them in the negative sense, but also in the positive sense. New experiences have the power to dislodge long-held beliefs and transform deeply rooted habits. He was getting the people to the place where they could do what He was asking them to do. He was building their muscle of faith. We know this from what is written in Deuteronomy 8:2: *Remember how the Lord your God led you all the way in the wilderness these forty years, to humble and test you in order to know what was in your heart, whether or not you would keep his commands.*

God still does this. He continues to build the faith muscle of His followers. Hebrews 12:7 says, *"Endure hardship as discipline; God is treating you as his children. For what children are not disciplined by their father?"*

Could God be using a current circumstance in your life to build your faith muscle?

At the end of Numbers, God announces his succession plan for Moses, who after forty years with these people, is close to death. Joshua is commissioned by the laying on of hands, as the Lord instructed Moses. The time of preparation has ended. The time to advance into the Promised Land has come.

What Will You Need for Your Journey?

Do you simply have a change of heart and that's it? No. For those that want to live the promised life, there are three commands, which are necessary to reset your thermostat. These become the new set point of your new mindset. No one really likes to get bossed around, but think about it this way: you are trusting God with your life so doesn't it make good sense to let Him tell you what you'll need to be successful?

A COMMAND IS SOMETHING TO BE OBEYED, AND OBEDIENCE IS A MATTER OF OUR WILL. WHETHER OR NOT JOSHUA WOULD BE STRONG, COURAGEOUS, OR OBEDIENT WAS DEPENDENT UPON HIS CHOICES.

You probably wear seat belts when you drive your car. Why? I wear seatbelts, but it may not be for the reason you may think. I wear one not because it's the law, although that is a good reason to do so. I made it a habit to wear my seatbelt before it was law. The reason I wear seatbelts is because I read the autobiography of Lee Iacocca and he said to wear one. If the guy that helped perfect and build the automobile recommended them, who am I to argue? Can you drive without wearing a seatbelt? Sure you can, but it's just stupid. Don't be stupid when you drive and don't be stupid with your life.

God told Joshua exactly what he needed to do, not just to be safe, but also to be successful and take possession of the land. To be successful in the promised life, you will need to be "all in" physically, emotionally, intellectually, and spiritually. God commanded Joshua to be strong, courageous, and obedient. With those three qualities, God would bring about His will in Joshua's life. The same is true for us. The big question is whether or not we trust God enough to choose strength, courage, and obedience.

Before we get into what each of these terms mean, let me ask you some questions. Are you strong? Are you courageous? Are you obedient...all the time? The good news is that you don't have to be all those things right now at this very moment. Apparently, God thinks you and I can choose to be strong, courageous, and obedient, just like Joshua. What's more, there seems to be a sense that these qualities do not happen accidentally; they must be chosen. A command is something to be obeyed, and obedience is a matter of our will. Whether or not Joshua would be strong, courageous, or obedient was dependent upon his choices.

These were not (and are not) optional qualities. They are foundational to being a monumental leader and living the promised life. They are three distinct qualities, yet, here they are interconnected. It is expected that all three will be present and actively work together. Let's take a closer look at these critical thermostat settings for entering the Promised Land and living the promised life.

Setting 1: Strength

Joshua had been a warrior for much of his life. When we meet him at the beginning of the story in the book of Joshua, he was ninety years old. I'm not sure how strong he was or could be but the command of God was pretty clear. "Be strong," He tells Joshua three times in seventy seconds. The word describes something done with great force. The Lord promised Joshua victory, but it would take effort on his part. Most good and noble adventures come with a certain amount of pressure and circumstances that turn up the heat. You can't produce diamonds without that though.

God's command to Joshua was simply to be strong. The people said they would follow Joshua and they encouraged him to be strong too. Maybe they had learned a thing or two during the forty years of wandering after all. Here's what the people told Joshua:

> *"Whatever you have commanded us we will do, and wherever you send us we will go. Just as we fully obeyed Moses, so we will obey you. Only may the Lord your God be with you as he was with Moses. Whoever rebels against your word and does not obey it, whatever you may command them, will be put to death. Only be strong and courageous!"* (Joshua 1:16b-18).

The phrase "be strong" is repeated to Joshua over and over again. "Be strong!" Moses told him (Deut. 31:7). "Be strong!" God told him (Josh. 1:6,9). "Be strong!" the people told him (Joshua 1:18). And again, Joshua was the warrior that led the battle against Amalek (See Exodus 17:9). He was selected as one of twelve spies that went into Canaan and came back with a positive report in the face of enormous peer pressure (See Numbers 13-14). And as we will closely examine, he was the leader who fought and defeated thirty-one kings throughout Canaan and only suffered one loss. Yet everyone is telling him to "Be strong!"

STRENGTH IS SOMETHING EVERY LEADER NEEDS, FROM PARENTS TO PRESIDENTS. IT'S ALSO SOMETHING EVERY FOLLOWER WANTS IN A LEADER.

It makes sense that people want to follow strong leaders. Strength is something every leader needs, from parents to presidents. It's also something every follower wants in a leader.

The opposite of strong is insecure, unreliable, weak, or vulnerable. Physically we must be present to be successful. Age and physical strength is not so much a factor as your choice to engage. We can choose to be strong. Decide now that you are going to show up and do what you can. Man or woman up. Play the man to the uttermost (no offense, ladies). Godly strength shows itself as confidence. It is seen in the way we walk and talk, and most of all, in the way we treat people.

Setting 2: Courage

Joshua lived by his convictions. Remember, he was almost stoned for standing firm on the belief that they could, and would, enter the Promised Land. God knew for Joshua to successfully navigate the promised life, he would need courage. God wanted him to stand firm and have deep resolve about what he was doing and why.

The verb "to be strong" and the verb "to be courageous" are synonyms. Using them together intensifies their meaning and impact, and creates a unique synergy that all leaders can't hear enough. God was calling for a full-court press. The teamwork of these two words forms a strong front. Like Joshua, effective Christian leadership requires courage on two fronts:

1) facing external conflict
2) facing the internal challenge of obedience

The context in Joshua 1 shifts back and forth between "bravery" and "determination." The first type of courage needed is to stand firm, or to be brave, when facing external conflict. *"No one will be able to stand against you"* (Josh. 1:5) and *"do not be afraid or discouraged"* (Josh. 1:9, NLT). Courage is not the absence of fear or doubt. It is doing what you know is right and believing God, even when it doesn't feel right and even when you feel afraid. Stand firm. Your feelings will catch up. Courage is the resolve to move forward, even when everything seems to be against you. Courage is possible when facing conflict because God is with you.

Then there is the courage needed to obey God. In this context, determination is the intended meaning. Obeying God's commands would require that Joshua be confident, resolute, and single-minded. Interestingly, this is of such importance that he is told to be *"very courageous."* Don't we all need to hear these words? I wonder how many leaders long to hear these words. Consider King David's encouragement to his son Solomon when he was faced with the ominous task of building the temple, the permanent house of God. David told him: *"Be strong and courageous and do the work..."* (1 Chron. 28:20). How often have we tried doing the work, but have forgotten the encouragement "to be strong" and "to be courageous"? How fired up would you be to hear these words spoken to you?

Hebrews encourages the believer to never give up his or her confidence in Jesus.

> *"Let us then approach the throne of grace with confidence, so that we may receive mercy and find grace to help us in our time of need"* (Hebrews 4:16).

> *"So do not throw away your confidence; it will be richly rewarded. You need to persevere so that when you have done the will of God, you will receive what he has promised"* (Hebrews 10:35-36).

DOUBT CERTAINLY CREEPS IN AS WE FACE OUR GIANTS AND FORTIFIED CITIES, BUT DOUBT NEED NOT CONTROL OUR ACTIONS.

Joshua was expected to be courageous regardless of how the situation might appear. Joshua would face giants and fortified cities where they were headed. You and I face the same as we travel with our families into the world and into the future. Giants are those people or things that seem like they could overtake us and conquer us. Fortified cities represent the things that we think are impossible because they *look* impossible. Doubt certainly creeps in as we face our giants and fortified cities, but doubt need not control our actions. Doubt is part of living. At times, you may doubt God or yourself. It happened to Joshua, and it happens to us too. Yet living the promised life requires the indispensable quality of courage. To be resolute means to be bold, persistent, serious, steadfast, tenacious and uncompromising. Joshua wasn't the only person commanded to be courageous. Jesus encouraged His followers to be courageous in the face of hardship too.

> *"But be of good courage: I have overcome the world"* (John 16:33, DARBY).

Like a winning coach, Paul finished a hard-hitting letter to the church in Corinth with these words: *"Be on your guard; stand firm in the faith; be courageous; be strong"* (1 Cor. 16:13).

Setting 3: Obedience

The third command and setting for our thermostat is obedience. In fact, God is very specific and careful to bring greater clarity to this by telling Joshua not to turn to the right or left. He is to be careful to obey all of God's law. The keys to Joshua's success was the same as those for a king: being rooted in God's Word rather than depending upon military might. This is why Joshua needed to be strong and courageous. Obeying God in every way is not an easy endeavor. Obedience is a choice we make.

Sometimes I think that the idea of commands-to-be-obeyed gets a bad rap in our culture. Yet it occurs to me that most success is a result of following rules. To win a war, commands must be followed. To win a legal case, rules must be adhered to in every step of the process from the investigation to the court and evidence procedures. When you drive, if you are to arrive alive, there are rules you'll need to obey. The adage "rules are made to be broken" sounds fine, until we seek justice. Then we claim everyone should play by the rules.

We're okay with having rules in our military, law or society, yet for some reason bristle at the thought of having rules to obey when it comes to individual and spiritual matters. "I'm against religion," some say. To which I reply, "Oh, really?" Just as there are consequences in every other area of life for ignoring the rules, so it is with our relationship with God. We do reap what we sow. Living the promised life requires not only strength and courage, but also obedience to God. Like it or not, these three qualities are inevitably and inexorably connected.

> LIVING THE PROMISED LIFE REQUIRES NOT ONLY STRENGTH AND COURAGE, BUT ALSO OBEDIENCE TO GOD.

In his last visit with the disciples after he rose from the dead, Jesus was *"teaching them to obey everything I have commanded you"* (Matt. 28:20b). Active obedience is critical. The only way to know if our faith is valid is by loving God and loving others. How do we love God? We obey Him. *"In fact, this is love for God: to keep his commands. And his commands are not burdensome"* (1 John 5:3).

The choice is yours.

All In

It might sound like I'm saying that everything is up to us: "Just have better mindset and everything will automatically change for the better." That's not what I believe. There is another extremely important part of the equation. Like two sides of a coin, there's our part and then there's God's part. Our part is to be "all in," fully committed, no outs, completely engaged and wholehearted. Did you know Caleb was commended by God for being wholehearted in Numbers 14:24?

While God required Joshua to be "all in" with strength, courage and obedience, he wanted Joshua to know that He was "all in" as well. God promised Joshua specific outcomes even before the first steps were taken into the promised life. How was God "all in"? We'll explore that next as we stop wandering and advance into the promised life.

Beliefs >> Thoughts >> Actions >> Habits >> Character >> Destiny

Joshua *believed* God's promise and *thought* taking the land was possible.
When the time came, he took *action* based on that belief. Courage,
strength and obedience became *habits* for him. Those habits defined his
character and led the Israelites into their *destiny* as
citizens in the Promised Land.

God believes you can be strong, courageous and obedient.
Do you believe in Him?

Look at your mindset. What are your set points?

Are you stuck in-between or are you wandering?

Are you prepared to advance?

Chapter 2

GOD IS FOR YOU!

"You did not choose me, but I chose you and appointed you so that you might go and bear fruit—fruit that will last—and so that whatever you ask in my name the Father will give you."

—John 15:16

Chosen

WE ADOPTED BOTH our wonderful kids—Micah and Ashley—at birth. Some grieve over the thought of not being able to give birth naturally, but Beth and I believe that, eight years into our marriage, it was God's will to build our family through adoption. Like all families we've had ups and downs, good times and bad, but through it all they are my kids and I love them. It's difficult for me to quantify just how much. We tell them, "You were born of our prayers."

When I got the call that Micah had been born, I was at my office, before the days of a cell phones. I did have a car phone, so I jumped in the car to go home, but was so excited that I drove in circles as I tried to get a hold of Beth and thought about what I needed from my office. I can recall details about each one. I remember the first time I held that six-pound, ten-ounce baby boy. It was love at first sight. At just two days old he stole my heart as I stared into his piercing blue eyes. From the beginning he has been alert, fun, energetic, curious, and loving—all qualities I love about him.

> HE WAS MY SON; I WAS HIS DAD AND HE WAS HOME.

As I held him, I experienced a kind of love that was new and that has grown deeper and richer through the years. Although I had taught about how much God loves us before this, in that moment I began to understand the sort of love for another that is totally and completely dependent on you. He was my son; I was his dad and he was home.

Then, two and a half years later, God brought Ashley into our lives. She was born on Easter Sunday, two weeks after her original due date. She has always taken her time and it has always been worth the wait. She had beautiful brown hair, brown eyes, and olive-colored skin. When I held her, she held me back. She melted into my arms. On Ashley's Gotcha' Day, the day we brought her home two days after her birth, the major news was a freak April Fool's Day blizzard in the northeastern United States that dumped rain, sleet, and snow from Maryland to Maine, leaving hundreds of thousands without power and as much as three feet of snow on the ground. But at the Holland house the major news was Ashley. Forgetting it was April's Fool Day, I called Beth to tell her the news of

> AS I HELD THEM I KNEW THAT I WOULD LOVE THEM AND PROVIDE FOR THEM, BUT THEY DIDN'T KNOW THAT.

Ashley's birth. I had to first convince her that this was *not* a cruel April Fool's joke. Before her birth, I was scheduled to speak in a citywide outreach halfway across the country. Because Ashley went past her original due date I canceled that speaking engagement. I wanted to be able to tell her and her brother that they have always been more important to me than even ministry and I'm glad that I did.

In a world of six billion people, only one boy is my son and only one girl is my daughter. As I held them I knew that I would love them and provide for them, but they didn't know that. "I love you more than anything in the whole wide world," I whispered in their little ears as I tucked them into bed each night. Micah, holding onto his pacifier with his teeth, would shorten "I love you" and say, "I...you." Ashley would say, "I love you mucho." To this day we can say or text, "Mucho!" and we know it means that's how much we love each other. Today our kids are adults, and I love them more now than the day they were born. Whatever life brings their way, whatever challenges they might face, I want them to know they can always count on me to do the best thing for them. I want them to know they are significant and my love is secure. It's mucho!

God also adopted us as His kids. John, the beloved disciple of Jesus, wrote, *"See what great love the Father has lavished on us, that we should be called children of God! And that is what we are! The reason the world does not know us is that it did not know him"* (1 John 3:1). We are His children. God wants even greater and better things for all of His kids, as I do mine. In fact, the more we come to understand and believe that God is for us, the more it will impact the way we think, and the more we will develop a healthy mindset. How you live is a direct response to how you think, and how you think is based on what you believe. Choose to believe the promises of God. Those promises are *for you.*

God Is *For* You

If you knew you couldn't fail, what would you do with your life? If you were promised success, what would you choose to do right this very moment? While it's vital that you and I understand that life's "not all about me," at some point we still wonder, *Will my life matter? Is what I am doing now worth it?* All of us have a fear of being insignificant and wonder if our lives have meaning. We want

> HOW YOU LIVE IS A DIRECT RESPONSE TO HOW YOU THINK, AND HOW YOU THINK IS BASED ON WHAT YOU BELIEVE.

to matter. We want to feel significant and secure. This is the part of the seventy-second speech that can easily be overlooked. Not only did God give Joshua a great pep talk and command to obey, God gave Joshua three enormous promises.

These promises still speak to the heart of every man and woman, especially leaders. They are as true for us today as they were to the Israelites four thousand years ago.

Some things are hard to believe, even if they are true. Take God's promises, for instance. They can be hard to believe: either because they have not happened yet, or because they are unusual or seem extreme. The resurrection was one of those things that was hard to believe, especially for those closest to Jesus. While all of His disciples struggled with doubt, Thomas was the last of the Twelve to believe. Jesus came to Thomas and said, *"Stop doubting and believe"* (John 20:27b).

God's Promises

Reread Joshua 1:1-9 again on page 6-7. This time pick up on the *promises* of God.

God promised Joshua three things: companionship, success and rest.

"I will be with you."

"You will be successful."

"I will give you rest."

I believe those three promises are monumental, as they address some of our life's greatest fears:

"Will I be alone?"

"Does what I do in life really matter?

"Will I be satisfied?"

God meets each one of these in the promises of Joshua 1.

God Promised Companionship

A pilot friend took me flying a few times. On one occasion, he invited me to fly to Titusville, Florida, to eat breakfast. On the way I recalled how much I enjoyed flying with my dad in a Cessna 172, a small plane with four seats. My friend asked, "You really used to do this?"

"My dad used to let me fly the plane. Well, he let me *think* I was flying the plane," I replied.

When airborne, Dad trimmed the plane out, and then invited me to fly. His hand was there all the time, near the controls. Both the pilot and copilot have the controls. Having my father with me gave me confidence that I could fly. The truth is I could not have flown without him next to me. Without him I would have lost confidence because I knew I was unable to takeoff or land the plane. Flying is what we did together. It's one of the ways Dad built my self-confidence, and I loved it.

God's charge to Joshua ends by reiterating words of encouragement and commitment: *"Have I not commanded you? Be strong and courageous. Do not be afraid; do not be discouraged, for the Lord your God will be with you wherever you go"* (Josh. 1:9). Joshua was not to fear or be discouraged because the Almighty God promised him He would be with him. The same is true for us. Why can we choose to be strong, courageous and obedient? Because God is with us. Even more than that, God is *for* us. He loves us and wants us to live well. In verse 5, God tells Joshua, *"as I was with Moses, so I will be with you: I will not fail you, or forsake you."* That must have been extremely reassuring and helpful for Joshua. He had experienced how the Lord had been with Moses through the plagues, parting the Red Sea, giving the Ten Commandments, receiving water from the rock, and much more. Joshua knew God.

When the Lord says He will be with us, He means it. How could Joshua lead with confidence in the battles that lay ahead? Every step he took into the Promised Land, he took with God at his side. Their first step in the Promised Land required crossing the Jordan River. This definitely required God's presence. Joshua could not have stopped the flow of the Jordan River, but God could. As they prepared to cross, the leaders of Israel instructed the people, *"'When you see the ark of the covenant of the Lord your God, and the Levitical priests carrying it, you are to move out from your positions and follow it. Then you will know which way to go, since you have never been this way before'"* (Josh. 3:3-4a). The ark, which represented God's presence, would lead them into their new life.

God promised Joshua that He would be with him, and God guarantees you the same thing. It's another God-sized guarantee.

God Wants to Be Close to Us and Moved into the Neighborhood

The entire Bible is a story of God drawing nearer and nearer to people, full of God's continuing promise of His presence in our lives. In Genesis 3:8, God walked in the garden with Adam and Eve, talking and meeting with them because human beings were created to be in fellowship with Him. Then sin broke their perfect relationship. God loved them anyway so He made clothing, or coverings, for them. However, their poor choice resulted in expulsion from the garden so they would no longer have access to the Tree of Life.

Rather than choosing to obey God in their new circumstances though, humankind continued a slow burn toward pursuing what he wanted rather than what God wanted. *"The Lord saw how great the wickedness of the human race had become on the earth, and that every inclination of the thoughts of the human heart was only evil all the time"* (Gen. 6:5). All except for Noah, who *"found favor in the eyes of the Lord"* (Gen. 6:8). Noah believed and obeyed God, even though others ridiculed him, and God established His covenant with Noah (Gen. 6:18).

Again, human beings attempted to make themselves great while God was in continual pursuit. God appeared to Abram (See Genesis 12) because He wanted to bless all nations of the earth. God was with Abram, and He fulfilled His promise to give him children. Issac was the son that fulfilled God's promise. Fast-forward to the exodus, when God sent Moses to deliver His people from Egyptian bondage. God was with His people and they could see that:

> *"By day the Lord went ahead of them in a pillar of cloud to guide them on their way and by night in a pillar of fire to give them light, so that they could travel by day or night. Neither*

the pillar of cloud by day nor the pillar of fire by night left its place in front of the people" (Exodus 13:21-22).

Next came the tabernacle, a mobile and temporary tent: *"So the cloud of the Lord was over the tabernacle by day, and fire was in the cloud by night, in the sight of all the Israelites during all their travels"* (Exo. 40:38). When the Israelites moved, as they often did in the wilderness, God's presence went with them, or more accurately, God's presence led them. Eventually Solomon built a permanent building called the temple, and God's presence dwelt there, among His people.

We can have an even greater confidence in God's companionship as Jesus is the continuing fulfillment of that promise: *"The Word became flesh and made his dwelling among us"* (John 1:14a). Jesus taught His disciples that He needed to leave so He could send the Holy Spirit. Human beings having the presence of God was so important that it was the last thing Jesus promised His followers before leaving the earth: *"And surely I am with you always, to the very end of the age"* (Matt. 28:20b). Because of Jesus' triumphant resurrection, we can have the Spirit of God within us as Counselor, Helper, and Friend. He indwells the body of Christ and is no longer limited to one location or building. Access to God does not depend on another person anymore.

ACCESS TO GOD DOES NOT DEPEND ON ANOTHER PERSON ANYMORE.

> *"Do you not know that **your bodies** are temples of the Holy Spirit, who is in you, whom you have received from God? You are not your own; you were bought at a price. Therefore honor God with your bodies"* (1 Corinthians 6:19-20).

Think about that: *"...your body is a temple of the Holy Spirit..."* His presence lives in you and me. That is how close He is—and wants to be with us.

God Promised Success

God promised Joshua that he would be *"prosperous and successful."* Reread Joshua 1:8 on page 7. What an enormous promise: "I will give you success." Wouldn't we all like to be promised that? Well, we are. No one wants you to be successful more than God does. Because we equate success with personal material wealth, success needs to be defined. To God, success is eternal and not measured by possessions. Kingdom success is about doing His will and trusting Him in our lives. If we accomplish His purpose, we are successful.

What is He saying to Joshua? It's the only time in the entire Old Testament these two words—prosperous and successful—are found together. The Hebrew root used here for "prosper" means "to prosper or succeed in one's endeavors." The second term is straightforward and means "to be successful." It is important to see this promise in its proper context.

The phrases that jump out in this verse are *"meditate on it"* and *"careful to do."* If Joshua ever wondered why God commanded him to be obedient, now he knew. Obedience wasn't an exercise in futility; obedience created the environment for God to fulfill His promises. Success wasn't merely the result of God being able. It was also the result of Joshua being obedient. The question is

> OBEDIENCE WASN'T AN EXERCISE IN FUTILITY; OBEDIENCE CREATED THE ENVIRONMENT FOR GOD TO FULFILL HIS PROMISES.

never God's ability; it's usually a question of my obedience. God's chosen leader and chosen people were to focus on knowing and obeying God's laws. That was the key to Joshua's success and it is the key to our success too. Let's take a look at a few of my favorite promises of God about living successfully.

Financial: *"You will be enriched in every way so that you can be generous on every occasion, and through us your generosity will result in thanksgiving to God"* (2 Cor. 9:11).

Wisdom: *"If any of you lacks wisdom, you should ask God, who gives generously to all without finding fault, and it will be given to you"* (James 1:5).

Forgiveness: *"If we confess our sins, he is faithful and just and will forgive us our sins and purify us from all unrighteousness"* (1 John 1:9).

Peace: *"The Lord is near. Do not be anxious about anything, but in every situation, by prayer and petition, with thanksgiving, present your requests to God. And the peace of God, which transcends all understanding, will guard your hearts and your minds in Christ Jesus"* (Phil. 4:5b-7).

Those are God-sized guarantees!

Biblically speaking, success is achieved because individuals seek the Lord earnestly and obey His commandments. This concept should not seem strange. Didn't your parents expect that using the family car was contingent on obeying the rules of the road and taking care of the car? Of course they did. And because they loved you, they allowed you to use the car to get to your first job. While you did that, they also expected you to drive the best you knew how.

> THE KEYS TO SUCCESS IN LIFE LIE IN BEING FOCUSED ON GOD AND IN CONSISTENT FAITHFULNESS TO HIM AND HIS REVEALED WORD.

Historically, in the book of Numbers, a new generation began to respond to God's voice. Their faith had been tested for forty years in the wilderness, and they were prepared to risk everything in the hope of something better. What they discovered is that when God's people lived in right relationship with Him, He fulfilled His promises. When they didn't live in right relationship with Him, He still loved them, but they wandered and life became difficult. The same, it can be said, is the case today: The keys to success in life lie in being focused on God and in consistent faithfulness to Him and His revealed Word.

How does God measure success? In a nutshell, success to God is choosing strength over fear, courage over discouragement, and obedience over personal desire. Whatever we do, we desire to be successful: as parents, in marriage, and in business. No one sets out to fail. The beginning point for living successfully is to believe God desires your success.

What do you seek? Some focus on money and seek affluence. Some focus on social media and seek to be noticed. Some focus on physical beauty and seek to be admired. Success is defined in different ways by different people. Be careful what you give up in the pursuit of what you want. True wealth is not found on a balance sheet. Jesus taught His followers: *"...seek first his kingdom and his righteousness, and all these things will be given to you as well"* (Matt. 6:33). Jesus also echoed the wisdom of Solomon: *"Trust in the Lord with all your heart and lean not on your own understanding; in all your ways submit to him, and he will make your paths straight"* (Prov. 3:5-6).

Do you know what that means? It means that while there may be obstacles or setbacks in life—such as mistakes, addictions, loneliness, bitterness, unforgiveness, anger, fear, or hurt — God will make a way for you to be prosperous and successful as you seek to please Him. Even Paul said his ultimate goal was to please God (2 Cor. 5:9).

God can help you reach the goals He has set for you. When you're tempted to believe otherwise, consider this promise:

> *"No temptation has overtaken you except what is common to mankind. And God is faithful; he will not let you be tempted beyond what you can bear. But when you are tempted, he will also provide a way out so that you can endure it"* (1 Corinthians 10:13).

God Promised Rest

Where does this promise come from? Is it even mentioned in Joshua 1:1-9? We must look backwards and forwards. Moses tells the people, *"But you will cross the Jordan and settle in the land the Lord your God is giving you as an inheritance, and **he will give you rest** from all your enemies around you so that you will live in safety"* (Deut. 12:10).

God made good on this promise in Joshua 22:1-4, seven years after they crossed the Jordan:

*"Then Joshua summoned the Reubenites, the Gadites and the half-tribe of Manasseh and said to them, 'You have done all that Moses the servant of the Lord commanded, and you have obeyed me in everything I commanded. For a long time now—to this very day—you have not deserted your fellow Israelites but have carried out the mission the Lord your God gave you. Now that the Lord your God **has given them rest as he promised**, return to your homes in the land that Moses the servant of the Lord gave you on the other side of the Jordan'"* (Joshua 22:1-4).

Isn't rest something we all long for? We grow weary fighting the battles of everyday life, let alone overcoming misfortune and adversity that come our way. The promise of rest is still available.

*"Therefore, since **the promise of entering his rest still stands**, let us be careful that none of you be found to have fallen short of it"* (Hebrews 4:1, emphasis added).

The promise of rest has been open since the time of creation and flows as a constant stream for us to drink from, if we will only stop to see and experience it. The only day of creation that never ended is the seventh day, the day of rest. On that day, there was a morning but no evening. That promise of rest has been open since God entered it according to Hebrews. Later we will talk about spiritual alignment in which we recognize the rhythms and pace of life needed to hear from God—and that includes rest.

Just as Joshua and the people experienced rest from war, we are promised rest from our battles and work. Thirty conquered armies and seven years later, Joshua received rest.

"So the Lord gave Israel all the land he had sworn to give their ancestors, and they took possession of it and settled there. The Lord gave them rest on every side, just as he had sworn to their ancestors. Not one of their enemies withstood them; the Lord gave all their enemies into their hands. Not one of all the Lord's good promises to Israel failed; every one was fulfilled" (Joshua 21:43-45).

To the Israelites, the promise of rest must have been good news after wandering in a desert for forty years.

Some Get Rest. Some Don't.

The writer of Hebrews goes on to describe that some will experience rest and others will not. Why?

"For we also have had the good news proclaimed to us, just as they did; but the message they heard was of no value to them, because they did not share the faith of those who obeyed" (Hebrews 4:2).

Faith is required to experience God's rest. Hebrews 11:6 says, *"And without faith it is impossible to please God, because anyone who comes to him must believe that he exists and that he rewards those who earnestly seek him."* There is no benefit in hearing and merely agreeing with this message. The promise of rest takes root when combined with

> REST IS NOT THE ABSENCE OF ACTIVITY OR EFFORT.

faith. Faith means trusting Him in all circumstances. Just as God won't force success or even His presence on His people, neither will He force His people to enter rest. Most things worth having in life require effort. Rest is not the absence of activity or effort. Hebrews 4:11 says, *"Make every effort to enter that rest."* We are being encouraged to do the work, to strive diligently. It sounds strange to say that entering rest requires effort, but faith demands action. Action is the evidence of faith. Although we are in Christ, we must put forth effort. As God's people assembled on the plains of Moab, preparing to enter Canaan, Moses reminded them their part in taking hold of the life God had planned for them. They had to make an effort to trust God to take possession of the Promised Land. Similarly, we make choices and act upon our faith to follow in Jesus' ways.

Israel had been denied entrance and therefore rest, because prior to this moment, they refused to accept the promise given to Abraham in entering the land. This wasn't a matter of injustice or of favoring one party or person over another. They were without excuse because they knew what God had said, but chose to disobey instead. Their unbelief turned into disobedience when the twelve spies returned from spying out the land. They knew God's Word but refused to obey it. A doctor can prescribe medicine but unless you willingly take it as prescribed, it is of no value. It's like having a gym membership but not using it.

Hebrews 4:3-7 continues to shed more light on rest:

> Now we who have believed enter that rest, just as God has said, "So I declared on oath in my anger, 'They shall never enter my rest.'" And yet his works have been finished since the creation of the world. For somewhere he has spoken about the seventh day in these words: "On the seventh day God rested from all his works." And again in the passage above he says, "They shall never enter my rest." Therefore since it still remains for some to enter that rest, and since those who formerly had the good news proclaimed to them did not go in because of their disobedience, God again set a certain day, calling it "Today." This he did when a long time later he spoke through David, as in the passage already quoted: "Today, if you hear his voice, do not harden your hearts."

We often apply this message to people on the outside of the Christian faith, but consider it as applied to the body of Christ. Don't harden your hearts. Before God created the world, He said, *"Today* if anyone would believe..." Today. How could that be possible? God is not limited by time. It is always today with God. If you are waiting for tomorrow, it will never come. Open your present. God is saying, "Don't harden your hearts. When you hear Me say something through My Word, believe it and put it into practice."

When we follow Jesus Christ, we experience peace, contentment, and security in God. Jesus said: *"Come to me, all you who are weary and burdened, and I will give you rest"* (Matt. 11:28, emphasis added). Feeling burdened and being tired is a fact of life. But when we follow Christ by faith we experience rest. This "rest" is different from the eternal rest we read about in Hebrews 3-4 because it begins immediately after we begin to follow Jesus. It is a sampling of the eternal rest that comes later. It's like walking through a food court at the local mall, sampling little bits of the food available, but never eating an entire meal. The meal will come later.

> DON'T HARDEN YOUR HEARTS. WHEN YOU HEAR ME SAY SOMETHING THROUGH MY WORD, BELIEVE IT AND PUT IT INTO PRACTICE.

Bearing fruit also is a result of being connected to Christ. John talked about it in terms of being connected to the vine, because we must be connected to him to bear His fruit (John 15). A vine does not work to bear its grapes. It does it naturally, drawing from the vitality of in the vine itself. We rest in God and as we dwell (or abide) in Him, we bear fruit.

Another way to open God's gift of rest is through prayer. *"Do not be anxious about anything, but in every situation, by prayer and petition, with thanksgiving, present your requests to God. And the peace of God, which transcends all understanding, will guard your hearts and your minds in Christ Jesus"* (Phil. 4:6-7). The experience of peace is a sign of rest.

Contentment + Thankfulness = Rest

Three Big Life Questions

Now that we've looked through the promises made to Joshua, let's look back at the big questions in life.

"Will I Be Alone?"

The simple straightforward answer is, "No, God is with you." We can believe that that's true, but you'll probably only know that it's true when He is all you have. In our world today we often think we are deeply connected only to find in a time of need that our connection is not what we thought it was. The reality for far too many is that we are all alone together. For example, the more we try to connect through social media platforms, the more alone we tend to feel. The strength found in knowing a few dependable friends is still the best way to go.

What we need is a growing awareness of the presence of Christ. He's always there. How do we cultivate this? I was at a point when my mentors stopped listening to me. That's when I realized I wasn't alone and that it'd be okay. Whenever people aren't listening anymore, it isn't a bad thing. That's what happened to me. I had some of the best, most capable mentors available and yet it wasn't until I was in solitude with God that I had peace.

> I HAD SOME OF THE BEST, MOST CAPABLE MENTORS AVAILABLE AND YET IT WASN'T UNTIL I WAS IN SOLITUDE WITH GOD THAT I HAD PEACE.

It's not being apart from people that makes the difference—it's being together with God. Communing with God and eating from His table in the Word of God helps us make decisions, gain insight, and know what we should do and when.

How do you know that God is for you? He promised to be with us, so He is. He proved it. God went all the way and gave His best. He gave His all. Because God gave His best for you, would He hold anything back? God graciously gives you *all* things. Why not concentrate on that, rather than your circumstances, trouble, heartache, or disappointment? In like manner, if God promised He would be with you, it makes sense to look for His presence.

God didn't hold out on you. Instead He gave Jesus up for us, the supreme act of love. The words "for us" indicate He stood in our place. The gift was graciously given. When God gives He does so without a grudging attitude. There isn't a sense that He's waiting for you to respond in like kind as if you can somehow repay Him. It is simply illogical to conceive that God would give His most treasured "possession"—His only Son—to secure your salvation, and then not also give everything else that is necessary to bring that salvation to completion.

There is a risk in living the promised life, and there is a need for real devotion and unshakable confidence in Christ and His presence. People fear they may be disqualified from God's love. We like to tell others that God loves them. How comfortable are you in saying, "God is for me" or "God loves me?" Choose to believe that God loves you. It's true, you know. He's not angry, and He doesn't love you because you stay busy doing good things for Him. God just loves you.

God's love is not conditional. We tend to think that unless I do _____ (fill in the blank), then God won't love me. Or God loves me except when I do this or until I do that. There are consequences for your decisions, but God loves you. We are accustomed to conditional love: "I'll love you if..." or "I'll love you when..." or even "I'll love you until...." It's difficult not to apply this mentality to our relationship with God because we think, *the better we are the more God loves us.* But God's love is radically different than conditional love. God's love can't be earned and it can't be returned.

"Does What I Do in Life Really Matter?"

The spotlight was turned on Mandy Harvey when she received the golden buzzer on *America's Got Talent* in June 2017; sending her straight to the live semi-finals. I met her when she was interviewed at our church. She talked about how her dream of being a choir teacher had been shattered when she lost her hearing. She thought: *Now what? Do I matter now? What do I do now?* Sometimes we think that when we're defeated, the right thing to do is to withdraw, especially when we're beaten. It happens to all of us. When we're doing well, we rarely ask, "Does what I do really matter?" We ask that question when we're defeated. That's the reality.

IT IS SIMPLY ILLOGICAL TO CONCEIVE THAT GOD WOULD GIVE HIS MOST TREASURED "POSSESSION"—HIS ONLY SON—TO SECURE YOUR SALVATION, AND THEN NOT ALSO GIVE EVERYTHING ELSE THAT IS NECESSARY TO BRING THAT SALVATION TO COMPLETION.

How can anyone understand the feeling of desperation and the confusing emotions Mandy experienced at that time? Her father, Joe, encouraged her to sing again. At first, she was timid about it. "Okay, I'll try it," she said, lacking confidence. She had to rely on someone else to tell her how she sounded when she sang. She had known how to sing and even when she lost her hearing, she could still sing. But she couldn't *hear* herself sing, so it felt like it was worthless and pointless.

By relying on others, trusting her pitch, and watching tuning machines, she now sings on key, and keeps time. Why? Because she remembered what it felt and sounded like to do so. We need to remember some things too. The Lord said to Joshua, "Remember, I was with Moses and I'll be with you."

Mandy's deafness didn't change, but her confidence did. Sometimes our circumstances don't change, but our confidence can. The Lord can give us confidence in any and all circumstances, but we tend to assess ourselves based on what we see, instead of trusting His promises to us and His presence with us. We ask the question about whether what we do matters or not at the wrong times—usually whenever we're feeling defeated, *not* when things are going well.

Because of my deep love for my kids, it would grieve me immensely if they did not live up to their potential. And God loves His kids more than that. The amount of love we have for our children pales in comparison to the love God has for each one of us. We cheer for our children and God cheers even more for us. Why wouldn't you make every effort to live up to your God-given potential? You and I don't live up to our potential whenever we forget, overlook, or ignore God's promises. The reason we can live fearlessly is because God loves us perfectly and eternally.

Every day God votes for you. Every day Satan votes against you. You cast the deciding vote. Every. Single. Day. You. Vote.

"Will I Be Satisfied?"

Sometimes what we believe will satisfy us and what will actually satisfy us are two different things. Satisfaction in life is something you choose rather than something you pursue. We have many choices: Contentment is a choice. Being thankful is a choice, and it is through these two areas that we show our love to God.

My dad is an example of someone who chose to be thankful and contented. He lived well and he died happy with his family around him. He was sixty-four years old. After serving nearly fifteen years in the Air Force, Dad made a career change and served as a minister in the church for thirty years. I once asked my dad if he ever regretted not retiring from the military. After all, only another five years and he could have been drawing retirement pay in addition to his current salary. Surely more money would have brought greater satisfaction. His answer surprised me.

He said he did not regret his decision to get out of the military when he did. While stationed in Germany, he fell in love with Jesus Christ, sitting under the teaching and example of Heinz and Ruth Mueller. What satisfied him changed; his beliefs solidified. Dad made a choice to fall in love with Jesus. As a result he broke his old patterns and habits. Why not decide now to live "all out" — with no regrets? How wonderful to be able to let go and smile again, and long before you are dying, live a life full of purpose and joy. Life is filled with choices. It is your life. Choose consciously. Choose to be content because contentment truly is a choice. Choose to live for Christ because He can enable and equip you to live intentionally.

During my dad's time in Germany, he became thankful for his salvation and felt indebted to Christ. When we are thankful, everything changes. When we are thankful in any given moment and in any circumstance, we can also be content. We can be satisfied. Dad left the military, and focused on the Lord. He never regretted not retiring from the military.

Whenever we choose to be content and thankful, we experience God's promised rest because they are signs that we trust Him. I am not talking about a life without hardship and pain. I am talking about finally resting in, and accepting, God's will for you, whatever the future on earth may hold. The apostle Paul chose contentment, and he certainly did not have a life without suffering. He suffered a lot. Paul also chose to be thankful. On the one hand, Paul accepted his circumstances as the will of God. On the other hand, he adapted his attitude and expectations according to what God was doing.

For the Israelites, crossing the Jordan River did not mean life on easy street. While the inhabitants of Canaan were afraid of the Israelites, they were not going to run away without a fight. The greatest battle the Israelites faced was not from the well-trained armies or the fortified cities in front of them, but from within as we will see. They had to choose to believe that God was for them, even when it seemed everything was against them.

A Growing Awareness of God's Presence

I can't overstate the importance of the promise of God's presence. *"If God is for us, who can be against us?"* (Rom, 8:31b). Paul presents this question to help us see beyond our circumstances. It's a statement more than a question. God promises He will not leave us like orphans, but will always be with us (See John 14:18). In the Book of Revelation we read that Christ walks among His church. As you take steps to live a life of faith, your greatest need in facing the challenges of life is an awareness of God's presence in your life! Your daily and growing awareness of the presence of Christ will prevent you from giving up and direct your steps. Daily decisions are made easier when He is with you.

What is coming against you right now?

What's got you down?

Are you experiencing doubt, disappointment, or loss?

Are you facing financial heartache, regret, remorse, or frustration?

It's not you against God, it's you and God against the world.

If God has your back, then why worry? Why be afraid? Regardless how hard things may seem at this moment, God is for

> AS YOU TAKE STEPS TO LIVE A LIFE OF FAITH, YOUR GREATEST NEED IN FACING THE CHALLENGES OF LIFE IS AN AWARENESS OF GOD'S PRESENCE IN YOUR LIFE!

you. The Christian's confidence is in God, and not circumstances. Let's look to our best example of confidence in God beyond circumstances: Jesus facing the cross. How did He do it?

> *"Let us fix our eyes on Jesus, the author and perfecter of our faith, who for the joy set before him endured the cross, scorning its shame, and sat down at the right hand of the throne of God"* (Hebrews 12:2).

I am an imperfect parent. Yet whenever one of my kids requests something I consider it carefully. I want to do what is best for them and would never intentionally do something to hurt them. In an even more personal way, God is with His children. Jesus compared God's involvement in our lives to our involvement in the lives of our children.

> *"If you, then, though you are evil, know how to give good gifts to your children, how much more will your Father in heaven give good gifts to those who ask him!"* (Matthew 7:11).

Our history has been one continuous story of God's movement to be closer to us. He is for us. He chose us and wants us to choose Him. He wants us to trust Him, to believe Him, to submit to Him, and to humble ourselves before Him. Take a lesson from those who have gone before us. When God's people live in right relationship with Him, He is with them. The promise of God is for everyone. That includes you and me.

My Rest

Do you remember my struggle with fellow leaders that I mentioned in the previous chapter? After four years of struggling, in a matter of seconds I had clarity and was ready to advance. You've probably heard the saying, "You sound like a broken record!" The truth is that the record of our sad circumstances isn't broken. We often tend to our pain by rehearsing it over and over in our minds, as well as to anyone who will listen. Like the Israelites complaining, the song is on repeat. It was time for me to take the needle off the record and enter God's rest and my promised life.

> MY REST CAME FROM KNOWING THAT WHATEVER CAME MY WAY, GOD WAS WITH ME.

Over the past several years I've matured and realized the way I framed the story assured that others, like my wife and mentors, would agree with me when they heard it. I've also come to realize that instead of working together, we were working against each other.

God led me to advance in my situation by submitting my resignation. I had expected to have a lifetime of ministry there, but God had different plans. I had to give up my dream for His. When I decided to make the move, I never told the story again until I wrote this book. In faith, we advance as we give up our dream scenario for His promised life.

Don't get me wrong; my promised life didn't come because I had a new assignment. On the contrary, my rest came from knowing that whatever came my way, God was with me. What story do you need to stop telling yourself and others, so that you can advance? Maybe it's dealing with a troubled relationship, rather than just talking to others about it. Maybe it's risking failure, and grabbing hold of a dream God has for you.

What can happen when we enter God's rest? We hear Him and see Him more clearly. Relationships flourish in rest and refreshing within our families. Let's make others dream of rest—God's rest. Regardless what is going on in your life right now, if you will trust Him, you will find His rest.

Three Days from Now

What do you want your life to look like three years, three months, three weeks or even three days from now? What dream do you need to seize for today?

When you come to a deep belief that God is for you, life can take on new meaning. Consider Paul's words in Romans 8:28-32:

> *"And we know that in all things God works for the good of those who love him, who have been called according to his purpose. For those God foreknew he also predestined to be conformed to the image of his Son, that he might be the firstborn among many brothers and sisters. And those he predestined, he also called; those he called, he also justified; those he justified, he also glorified. What, then, shall we say in response to this? If God is for us, who can be against us? He who did not spare his own Son, but gave him up for us all—how will he not also, along with him, graciously give us all things?"*

Similarly, Joshua 1 ends with a resounding battle cry as the people answer Joshua that they will follow him into the Promised Land and fully obey the Lord, repeating the words God had said to Joshua: *"Only be strong and courageous!"*

Both the words in Romans and Joshua 1 remind me of the movie *Home Alone*. We don't always feel like a brave warrior, but God can do something with us even if we feel more like eight-year-old Kevin McCallister. As he hides under the bed, Kevin says to himself, "This is ridiculous. Only a wimp would be hiding under the bed. And I can't be a wimp. I'm the man of the house."

You aren't a wimp! You are a child of God and He is for you. Stand on the front porch and declare: "Hey, I'm not afraid anymore! I said, I'm not afraid anymore. Did you hear me? I'm not afraid!"

We are not alone, we have a mission that He will help us accomplish, and it will be the most fulfilling thing we have ever done. That's about as good as it gets!

Beliefs >> Thoughts >> Actions >> Habits >> Character >> Destiny

Joshua believed God's promise and thought taking the land was possible. When the time came, he took action based on that belief. Courage, strength and obedience became his habits. Those habits defined his character and led the Israelites into their destiny as citizens in the Promised Land.

God promised that He is with you — right now. Do you believe that He is?

In what areas are you successful right now in your life?

Are you learning to be content in any and all circumstances?

Are you learning to be thankful in any and all circumstances?

Journal about a time of trial in which God met you.

Chapter 3

MONUMENT ONE: REMEMBER WHAT GOD HAS DONE: YOUR FUTURE DEPENDS ON IT.

"I will remember the deeds of the Lord; yes; I will remember your miracles of long ago."

—Psalm 77:11

A New Beginning

EVER HAVE A moment when time just seemed to stand still? You've felt great anticipation building up to an event, then suddenly the day came and you realized, "Woah! It's happening. What I've been waiting for all this time is actually happening!" Maybe it was your wedding day, the moment your first child came into the world, the first day of your dream job, or the day you launched that business you've worked toward for years. Time seemed to stand still and you were almost in disbelief that it was actually happening.

You have a gold ring to commemorate your wedding day and remember your marriage covenant. You save the hospital band or blanket, or carefully tuck the first set of footprints into a baby book to remember them. Maybe you framed the first dollar you earned from the new business. You don't want to forget that momentous day.

The crossing of the Jordan River was that kind of day for Joshua and many of the Israelites. He and Caleb had dreamed of this day nearly a half-century earlier when they first set eyes on the Promised Land. While most monuments and memorials are built years or decades after an event has taken place, this first monument of stones Joshua built was constructed as the event happened. What an encouragement and affirmation this must have been. In essence, God told them, "You're going to want to remember this! You will get to the other side and you will have victory because your descendants are going to see these very stones you are about to carry across."

As Joshua stood in the middle of the river, finally and faithfully claiming the promises of God, the sense of destiny must have been overwhelming. The last time the Hebrews had lived in the land was about 500 years before, when Jacob raised his twelve sons there. Now his twelve sons returned to the land as one nation. It is significant that this happened on the tenth day of the first month. This is exactly forty years to the day since Israel marched out of Egypt. They had completed their journey back from a life of bondage to a new life of freedom. They were moving into the Promised Land that God had earmarked for them.

> AS JOSHUA STOOD IN THE MIDDLE OF THE RIVER, FINALLY AND FAITHFULLY CLAIMING THE PROMISES OF GOD, THE SENSE OF DESTINY MUST HAVE BEEN OVERWHELMING.

> On the tenth day of the first month the people went up from the Jordan and camped at Gilgal on the eastern border of Jericho. And Joshua set up at Gilgal the twelve stones they had taken out of the Jordan. He said to the Israelites, "In the future when your descendants ask their parents, 'What do these stones mean?' tell them, 'Israel crossed the Jordan on dry ground.' For the Lord your God dried up the Jordan before you until you had crossed over. The Lord your God did to the Jordan what he had done to the Red Sea when he dried it up before us until we had crossed over. He did this so that all the peoples of the earth might know that the hand of the Lord is powerful and so that you might always fear the Lord your God" (Joshua 4:19-24).

After crossing the river, the Israelites went to a place called Gilgal to make their camp. Gilgal, which means "the reproach has been rolled away," was near

Jericho. Forty years of spiritual defeat and failure had been rolled away—the past was behind them. God had been faithful to His promise. They had arrived at a new beginning in a new land. The days of aimless wandering in the wilderness were behind them. Now they were living a new life in a new place. Forty years had taught them that they could trust God. They were now a people with a powerful new sense of purpose, determined to take new territory with God.

Acknowledging this occasion was not merely pomp and circumstance or a time for a commemorative plaque. This monument, and all the other monuments to come, are important because history does repeat itself. The same principles that governed Israel are still at work as God continues to write History. Remembering mattered because...

It Was Imperative to Their Future.

They were to begin this journey into the promised life with the end in mind. The purpose of the monument is clearly stated:

> *"He did this so that all the peoples of the earth might know that the hand of the Lord is powerful and so that you might always fear the Lord your God"* (Joshua 4:24).

As with other memorials in the Old Testament, the intention was to provoke questioning, especially from future generations. Many of the memorials in the Old Testament served a specific purpose. God warned Israel not to let the environment of the pagan society that surrounded them dictate their values. This pile of stones was a memorial to that, a reminder of God: the Father, the Caregiver, and the Performer of miracles, and how He had provided the way for His people to enter the land He had promised to them.

The decisions and actions made on this day would impact those who came after them and they were to make sure of it. God intentionally wants the past to inform the future. Remembering God's faithfulness and power should cause our future children and grandchildren to replace improper fear with faith.

The Do-Over

Have you ever been given a do-over? Maybe it was during a round of golf and you called a mulligan, or perhaps it was during a kickball game when you were in school. The gym teacher felt sorry for you and allowed a do-over. Our faithful leader, Joshua, has been entrusted and empowered by God to lead in one of the best do-overs in all of history.

Israel had been in this "crossing over" situation before. At the Red Sea, God dried up the land, so the entire nation could cross, escaping the Egyptians and moving closer to the Promised Land. What an amazing, life-changing experience that must have been. Or at least one would think.

How quickly they developed amnesia. It was only a short journey from Egypt to Canaan by the most direct route. An impressive highway of about 250 miles ran up the coast through the country of the Philistines. Within a month or so of God's faithful and powerful Red Sea rescue, they sent spies to scout out the Promised Land—their next momentous crossing. We know how that turned out. Everyone was afraid to cross and the little band of leaders were almost stoned for even suggesting it. No wonder the first thing God wanted them to do after they finally crossed the Jordan River was build a monument. It was a monumental moment!

Fear or Faith?

While the crossing of the Red Sea and the Jordan River might seem similar, only one was monument-worthy. The difference between the two crossings is simple. All that was needed to cross the Red Sea was a little faith because they feared the weapons of the Egyptians more than the dry ground and walls of water. Sometimes, from the outside looking in, we can take a step forward and it looks like big faith, when in reality, it is a tiny bit of faith with a whole lot of fear lying underneath the surface—a jailhouse conversion.

But monumental faith was required to cross the Jordan River. This time the enemy was in front of them, not behind. They were not being pursued and didn't feel threatened. It is one thing to flee from the past, the Devil and death. It is quite another to advance into enemy territory with all its giants and fortified cities. Perhaps it is possible to have enough faith to see us through redemption (from Egypt) but not take us into abundant living (Canaan). They could be driven like cattle through the Red Sea, but they had to follow like sheep to cross the Jordan River.

The first time the Israelites faced that Jordan River, they just couldn't do it. After the twelve spies returned and reported to Moses, that river became a stone wall which reached into the heavens and was as long as the ends of the earth and that stopped them from crossing.

Stay Focused. Don't Let Your Purpose Be Hijacked.

Fear has a way of hijacking our minds and our purpose. The first time the spies were sent in by Moses, they were not focused on the joy set before them, except for Caleb and Joshua. The spies lost focus. In my tae kwon do training, I've been learning about focus. The thing that stands out to me most is that in both tae kwon do and life, we should always be willing to give a little more than is required or expected. To do that, you must learn to concentrate on what you know with your mind, rather than what you see with your eyes.

WE SHOULD ALWAYS BE WILLING TO GIVE A LITTLE MORE THAN IS REQUIRED OR EXPECTED. TO DO THAT, YOU MUST LEARN TO CONCENTRATE ON WHAT YOU KNOW WITH YOUR MIND, RATHER THAN WHAT YOU SEE WITH YOUR EYES.

One of the first real tests that a martial artist faces is the test of breaking a board. Each time a student begins to learn how to break a board, we instruct them to kick beyond the board or through the board. To help him or her grasp this concept, we remove the board so the student is able to visualize the point which they should strike. The goal is for them to concentrate their focus, energy, power, and aim beyond the fictitious barrier.

Most students do well in this exercise. Then comes the actual test. Everything changes the moment they see an actual board standing in the way. At that point something happens in the mind of the student. Rather than concentrating on kicking beyond the board, their full attention is captured and placed on the board itself. The board is obstructing their perfect view of their goal. What seemed possible now feels impossible.

Why does that happen? Why will a student agree to concentrate kicking to one point, practice kicking to that point, and then—somewhat unconsciously— lose sight of their goal? Why do they become in danger of fixating on the board? Is it that the student doesn't trust their instructor? I think the explanation is a rather simple one. This change of focus happens because the board is real. Breaking the board was a nice goal, but breaking through the board is another matter entirely. What the student knows in their mind and believes in their heart is hijacked by what they see with their eyes. They believe their instructor, but then they begin to think: that is the problem. It seems that the more they think about the board, the more they stop believing they can break it.

That is a powerful life lesson. You may know there is more than what you might be able to see in this life and so you make your goal to live with faith, courage, and determination. Yet, sometimes whenever you face physical, rela- tional, or financial obstacles, to name a few, your hope, faith, and joy is hidden from sight. Then what happens? You focus on the problem rather than beyond the problem to the solution. You focus on what may become a source of pain rather than the joy that lies just beyond it. In some instances you may find you have been fixated on the "board" in your life for years.

Because you have lost sight of the goal, you may continually—and coura- geously—kick against that very real obstacle. This just hurts again and again. Why are we afraid of the trouble we face? There is no simple answer, but it might be because of a simple loss of sight. It seems to me that in the same way a student might be afraid of seeing the board, although he or she knew there would be a board to break, we can be afraid in life.

We don't want to cause ourselves unnecessary pain and suffering, so we do everything in our power to avoid the pain we expect. We want to break the board, but we don't want it to hurt. We want to move through each challenge without suffering in any way. Yet suffering leads to perseverance, perseverance leads to character, and character leads to hope, according to Romans 5:3-5.

Something powerful happens in the human spirit when we focus our attention and belief on something that is outside of ourselves and beyond our trouble. For me, whenever I focus my attention on Christ and eternal life, both of which are beyond anything on this earth, I also find exceptional joy and abiding peace. And when I focus on joy, I am better able to break through the obstacles that life presents. Not always without pain and not always on the first try.

Wilderness Christianity or Abundant Living?

Have you taken a small step of faith, like running across the Red Sea, and don't want to return to a former habit or way of life? Has fear caused you to stop short—hijacked you—of true freedom in Christ, crossing over into the promised life? Don't settle for wilderness Christianity.

In Joshua 14, Caleb looked back with Joshua and remembered their time as spies. He said: *"I was forty years old when Moses the servant of the Lord sent me from Kadesh Barnea to explore the land. And I brought him back a report according to my convictions, but my fellow Israelites who went up with me made the hearts of the people melt with fear. I, however, followed the Lord my God wholeheartedly"* (Josh. 14:7-8).

What is making your heart melt with fear? Is there something you want to do, but are afraid to put your whole heart into it because, well, what if it fails? Faithful leaders, like Caleb and Joshua, follow the Lord wholeheartedly, risking failure and even death. I have to believe finally crossing the Jordan River had a beautiful, sweet satisfaction that meant more to them than anyone else. While the rest of the Israelites had been wandering in the wilderness, Joshua and Caleb had been waiting for this very day. I think this crossing and its subsequent monument-building was a highly personal time of worship with the Lord for Joshua. The Bible says Joshua set up a second monument, in the dry river bed where the priests had been standing with the ark of the covenant before the waters returned, *"and they are there to this day"* (Josh. 4:9). Monumental leaders who take risks are gifted with treasured moments like that sometimes. That sounds like abundant living to me. Jesus wants the same for you.

> *"I have come that they may have life, and have it to the full!"*
> (John 10:10b).

Ten Leadership Highlights

There are many life and leadership lessons within chapters two through six of Joshua—enough that those chapters could be an entire book in and of itself. We meet Rahab, who is in the lineage of Jesus and there is the battle of Jericho, which is probably the story and battle for which Joshua is best known. While I want to focus on the monuments, this chapter would be incomplete without recognizing at least some of the additional leadership principles modeled for us here. This chapter can mark your opportunity to build Joshua's first monument in your own life. In the pages that follow you will find many thought-provoking questions. Don't rush through them. Get out a journal and apply them to your life as you read. Let those answers guide you into the promised life.

1) Leaders Investigate Where They Are Going

Before entering this new, promised life, Joshua had a clear strategy. The Israelites investigated where they were going; only this time around, they sent only two spies into the land. It's a good thing to look before you leap, but I need to warn you not to spend all your time making the perfect plan because it doesn't exist. Thinking about taking your first step is not the same as taking the first steps. Until you start, you can't finish. Moab, where they had been living, was close to Canaan but it wasn't Canaan. Don't live around the edges of your dreams. It doesn't matter what you know. If you know lots of information, but do not combine it with faith, it is worthless. Hebrews 4:2 says the Israelites heard the good news but it was not of value to them because they did not combine it with faith. Thus they did not enter God's rest and the promised life the first time.

Is there some research you need to do to prepare for your promised life?

2) Leaders Take Care of Unfinished Business

Before Israel fought a battle in Canaan, they stopped to take care of some unfinished business. Sometimes so must we. As they prepared to cross the Jordan River, Joshua told the people, *"Consecrate yourselves, for tomorrow the Lord will do amazing things among you"* (Josh. 3:5). While consecration is an ongoing process, there are times we need to step up and prepare for an "all in" commitment: physically, emotionally, and spiritually. Fresh starts and the ability to see miracles often require us to be "all in" with nothing blocking our view: behind or in front.

When have you been "all in" for something?
What does it look like to be giving your best self to the Lord?
Do you have some unfinished business with the Lord or others?

3) Leaders Go First, So Be Willing to Get Your Feet Wet

Unlike some of the movies we've seen where the king or general hangs back and sends the troops ahead, leaders go first. I'm a huge Indiana Jones fan. One of my favorite moments in the saga of Dr. Henry Jones's fictional life is his leap from the lion's head in the quest for the Holy Grail. Indiana's father has been injured and he wants to find the grail, hoping it will save his father's life. Time is running out. Our great adventurer is walking through a tight rock canyon and comes to an opening, revealing that he is on the edge of a great cliff with a huge abyss between him and the opening on the other side. He consults his father's notebook about the Knights of the Round Table who are said to have protected the grail. He reads, "Only a leap from the lion's head will prove his worth."

"Impossible. Nobody can jump that," Indiana mutters to himself.

Then he has a revelation: "It's a leap of faith!"

With his hand on his heart and his foot in the air, Indiana takes the fateful (or is it faithful?) step. It's only after he steps that he can see the rock bridge under his feet, spanning the ravine. He smiles with that iconic half-smirk and hops to the other side.

Like Indiana Jones, the priests had to take the first steps into the raging Jordan River and in that leap of faithful leadership, the waters were pushed back. But the priests took the step first. The Rev. Martin Luther King, Jr. is quoted as saying, "Faith is taking the first step even when you don't see the whole staircase."

Are you willing to take the steps God places in front of you, even if you can't see the entire staircase?

4) Leaders Don't Get Ahead of God

Sometimes we, in a desire to "do great things for God," run ahead of Him. In most instances, God views this as disobedience. We need to remember that Israel once tried to take Canaan in their own power. Forty years earlier Moses told the Israelites the consequence of their unbelief in receiving the reports of the spies was that they would have to wander in the wilderness for forty years. The next morning the Israelites decided to take Canaan with or without God. That did not go well for them. Do you have a habit of getting ahead of yourself or God? Some people are more prone to this than others. If this sounds like you, read Numbers 14 and see what happened to the Israelites.

But forty years later, with Joshua closely following the exact instructions from God, the Lord led the way. The Ark of the Covenant represented God's presence, His throne. The priests were to carry the Ark across first, and stand obediently in the center of the Jordan. There also was to be space between the people and the Ark because of the holiness of God.

How can you recapture a reverence for God so that you can stay in step with the Spirit in your promised life?

5) Before Battle, Leaders Make and Break Habits

Change can be terrifying and painful. Israel had lost sight of some of the habits created to draw them closer to God and make them a people set apart. After crossing the Jordan River, circumcision was reinstated, as well as observing the Passover. At Gilgal, where Joshua constructed the monument and the people camped in their new promised life, they had to remove disobedience and remove things not in God's will. Without new habits, they likely would not last. It was important that they did not forget their destiny as God's chosen people. In observing the Passover, the people established a new rhythm to go with their fresh start. It was a change of heart on the inside as well as a change in rituals and habits on the outside. They were not going to live their lives, seeing just how far they could walk away from God and still be okay. Now, they made it their intent to walk near Him. What about you? Are you walking as closely to the Lord as you know how?

The Israelites also stopped some things. They had a manna mentality, living temporarily with all they needed handed to them. This new life required them to work hard to achieve success. It was time to make a permanent home, and now they had to eat from the land. God no longer fed them. The cloud they had followed also was gone. They would have to follow God by faith without constant "visible" guidance. It was time for Israel to grow up and mature in their faith—as I said earlier. This was monumental faith.

It is true that we are creatures of habit, but we get to CHOOSE our habits. What habits do you need to make? Which ones should you break?

6) Leaders Give God the Glory

Moses had just commissioned Joshua to take over. As a new leader, it would be tempting for Joshua to subvert His power. After all, Joshua had been waiting for this moment for forty long years because of someone else's unbelief. Joshua could have said, "I told you so!" But he did not. He followed God's instructions completely, humbly, and with resolve. The monument built at Gilgal was to remind the Israelites, and Joshua, that God should get all the credit for the miracles already accomplished as well as the miracles and victories to come. Leaders recognize where the true source of power comes from and give God credit, both privately and publicly. Even at the end of his time in leadership, Joshua continued to give God the glory for what He had done.

> LEADERS RECOGNIZE WHERE THE TRUE SOURCE OF POWER COMES FROM AND GIVE GOD CREDIT, BOTH PRIVATELY AND PUBLICLY.

Have you had any victories lately? How have you deliberately given God the credit?

7) Expect the Unexpected

God delights in using strange methods to achieve great things. In Joshua 2, He used Rahab—a prostitute—to inform and protect the spies. Then God used trumpets to crumble the walls of Jericho. This is His nature—always keeping us on our toes. He enabled Samson to win a victory over the Philistines by wielding the jawbone of a donkey. He enabled David to slay Goliath with a sling and a stone. Centuries later, God selected an ordinary Jewish girl to bring His Son into this world, and He selected tiny Bethlehem as the place for Him to be born. Learn to expect the unexpected from our holy and powerful God.

The supreme example, of course, is the cross of Christ. It seems ridiculous to suggest that a Jewish rabbi dying on a Roman cross would provide eternal salvation for sinners. But that cross, so despised and scorned, is the means that God chose for saving sinners. That cross would prove to be a stumbling block to the Jews and a laughingstock to the Greeks, but to those who are saved, it is both the power and the wisdom of God (See 1 Corinthians1:18–25). Why did God choose such a strange means of salvation? So all the glory for the salvation of sinners would be given to Him (See 1 Corinthians 1:26–31). These unexpected, miraculous means remind us to give Him the glory for what He does. Believe that God knows best, especially when God uses strange methods to achieve great things through you.

When have you seen God use the unexpected for His purposes and glory?

8) Do the Easy Things

Once inside the Promised Land, the first thing that confronted Joshua was the battle which lay before him. The walls around Jericho were several yards thick and each one was twelve-to-fifteen feet high. Jericho had one wall inside another built on a hill, and those walls towered from eight-to-ten stories high. Inside were well-armed and fiercely warlike people. What Joshua saw with his eyes was a giant of immense proportions. Yet, God didn't ask them to have target practice with their arrows, perfect their swordsmanship, or construct catapults to take down the doors and scale the walls. He said, "March."

Do the easy things. Not everything in the promised life is hard or difficult. Walk around the city? Yeah, we are going to walk around the city once a day and then have dinner. Just walk around the city? Why do something that easy when the battle is more difficult than that? March, because God said so. Period.

Not everything in following God is hard, so do the easy things! There are big results from doing the easy things. Get up and have a quiet time. Go to church every week. Meet with the sick. Pray for one another. Do what God tells you to do.

What easy things could you be doing right now to be more obedient to God's call on your life?

9) Risk Exposure

In Utah is the little town of Moab. Interestingly, it was named after the biblical land where Israel camped as they prepared to enter Canaan. According to the town's website, early Mormon settlers in the 1800s saw similarities between the two locations. Physically, the region was a green, fertile valley in the middle of a desert.

On a recent trip to Moab, Utah, Greg, a friend, learned an important lesson about exposure. An avid hiker, he had climbed great elevations with no problem as long as he had something to lean against. However, when he faced a forty-five-degree climb on a ridge with nothing to lean against, he sat on the aptly named Chicken Rock and waited a while before moving forward. Later, Greg explained this ridge to an owner of a hiking shop nearby. The shop owner knew the location my friend described, and explained the concept of exposure. Exposure means you are on a steep slope with little or no protection from a fall. Hiking trails are classified by degree of difficulty in regards to the amount of exposure faced.

> NOT EVERYTHING IN FOLLOWING GOD IS HARD, SO DO THE EASY THINGS!

The shop owner told Greg that when he got to this ridge there was a thirty mile-per-hour wind, so, unlike Greg, he didn't cross it. Like these hikers, Joshua also faced complete exposure. Now they had entered enemy territory and walking around the walls of Jericho totally exposed them to the enemy for six days. What if God didn't do what He said He would, and Joshua failed? As exposure increases, so does risk. At this point in Joshua's experience, the faith of the people had been tested and they were prepared to fight through the fear of exposure and focus their faith on God. The concept of exposure is especially true for leaders. If you want to live the promised life, you must go beyond what used to scare you.

> IF YOU WANT TO LIVE THE PROMISED LIFE, YOU MUST GO BEYOND WHAT USED TO SCARE YOU.

If you are a leader, you will have to face exposure. Are you okay with that? What kind of exposure scares you the most?

What risks might you have to take in order to lead yourself and others into the promised life?

10) Lead into the Future

This first monument might look like just a strange pile of ordinary stones from an outsider's point of view, but it wasn't. Our lives can look like that too. When people don't know our story, we look ordinary, but if we share what God has done in us, our very lives have the power to point people to Jesus, just like the monument.

Just as Joshua had monumental moments that wove his story into God's story, so do I. Mine are not stones piled by a river, but memories of the people and moments that helped build me and my faith. Certain places remind me of God's work in my life. One such place is Winslow, Arizona, where I spent my formative years. I will always remember the church there with its fold-down theater seating. It was my father's first church and one of my jobs was to clean out the baptistry. It was made of rocks and I was baptized in it. Our family really thrived in that place.

I also remember certain people who were formative to my faith and told me truths about myself. I attended the Institute of Practical Ministry (IPM) in the late 1980's under Dr. Gary Beachamp. He told me the truth and loved me enough to take me to a better place. He was the senior minister of a megachurch and it was the final part of the program. You had to be invited back for the residency program for the second year. He called me into his office with a view overlooking downtown Dallas. The meeting was less than ten minutes but I'll never forget it. He got right to the point.

"You know what your problem is, Dan. You lack confidence," said Dr. Beachamp.

I snickered, thinking, "That is what I don't lack!"

But there was a pause—enough for me to really hear what he said. There was something in the way he said it that I knew he was telling me a truth about myself.

He continued in his thick Texas drawl, "I want to invite you back to the residency program. You know what? We are going to work on that. Yep. We are going to work on that. We sure are."

And that was it. I shared the meeting details with my wife and she asked me, "Doesn't that make you mad? You are one of the most confident people I know!"

"Beth, I think he told me the truth. I think something new is going to happen," I said.

Then there was Dr. Claude Reynolds. As I prepared to attend the IPM in Dallas, Texas, Dr. Reynolds, one of the church elders, called and asked to come by my office. He sat down in front of my big old Texas-sized desk, and said, "God's given you great abilities. I can see it, and you are really good at what you do. There is a danger though. Because you are so good, you are going to be tempted to lean on your talents, instead of sharpening your skills. Don't lean on your talents. Sharpen them."

Again, I could have been offended, but I wasn't. I knew he was telling me a truth. Those two short meetings had a huge impact on me. They literally led me to live differently, and changed the trajectory of my faith and leadership. I'm sure Moses told Joshua many things over their years in the desert together that impacted Joshua's faith and leadership.

I share these with you, hoping to get you thinking...

Who has spoken truths to you?

Look back and identify those monumental moments where God has already seen you through, spoken to you, or spoken through others to you. Record them. Speak them out loud. Share those truths with those who are coming after you. Intentionally point people to the powerful God working in and through you. It doesn't take long for people to move far away from God—to forget who He is and what He has done.

Joshua's name was originally Hoshea. The faith we see in Joshua has been carved out over a lifetime. I cannot help but wonder if his parents had a vision for freedom, not only for their family, but also for their nation. I think that is a plausible theory since they named their son Hoshea, which means "sal-

> ALWAYS REMEMBER WHO REALLY SAVES THE PEOPLE — GOD DOES.

vation." I picture the parents asking, "What shall his name be?" Someone says, "Hoshea." "Perfect. His name is Hoshea," and no further discussion would have been needed.

Somewhere along the journey from Egypt to the edge of the Promised Land, Moses changed Hoshea's name to Joshua. "Salvation" became "Yahweh saves." Joshua's name is monumental. Always remember who really saves the people — God does. It's our responsibility, like it was the Israelites, to share the story of what God has done with the next generation.

As the Israelites crossed the Jordan and watched the walls of Jericho crumble, there was a sense that history had been flowing toward this moment. But we know the story didn't stop there. It continued and Joshua is a foreshadowing of the Savior to come, Jesus Christ. The story of the Bible is, in a word, "salvation." If it were a play, the director would be God, and Jesus would be the main character.

God told Abram that his descendants would inherit the land of Canaan and it was happening, although nearly 500 years later. How can this be? God understands time in linear terms just as we do. Yet unlike us, God lives outside of time. He works within time without being limited by it. We live within time and are confined by it because we are created beings, and not immortal. Scripture says that time is flowing ultimately toward the second coming of Jesus. God, who created the notion of time, also controls the events in time. Therefore, *"when the fullness of time had come, God sent forth his Son, born of woman..."* Paul wrote in Galatians 4:4, ESV. Because the

> IF WE WILL FOLLOW THE DIRECTION GOD GIVES IN THIS FIRST MONUMENT AND WE TELL OUR CHILDREN WHAT GOD HAS DONE, HIS STORY IS TIMELESS.

story is about salvation, we must learn to tell the story of our life in Christ. We must lead into the future and though we are bound by time, we don't have to be limited by it. If we will follow the direction God gives in this first monument and we tell our children what God has done, His story is timeless. Every leader, from president to pastor to parent, has the responsibility to pass along the story of God's power and His salvation.

> *"In the future when your descendants ask their parents, 'What do these stones mean?' tell them, 'Israel crossed the Jordan on dry ground'"* (Joshua 4:21).

Beliefs >> Thoughts >> Actions >> Habits >> Character >> Destiny

Do you believe God has saved you?

Do your thoughts and actions align with that belief?

Are you being driven by fear or are you following by faith?

Chapter 4

MONUMENT TWO: YOU MUST DEAL WITH TROUBLE

"Endure hardship as discipline."

—Hebrews 12:7

Six-Year-Old Thug

DO YOU REMEMBER the first time you made a conscious choice to break the rules and disobey your parents or a teacher? I do. I was six years old and living in Lubbock, Texas. Three houses away on the corner of 35th Street and Memphis Avenue, a wrecking ball was tearing down a red brick house. I was instructed, very explicitly, not to go down there. I was allowed to watch from my yard only.

Eventually, I ended up going down there. The temptation was simply too strong for my six-year-old thug self to resist. Before long, I found myself throwing pieces of brick across the road. I got pretty good at hitting the other side of the road. I needed a harder challenge. I thought I should try and throw the bricks over cars and hit the other side. Just as I could see the whites of the driver's eyes, I launched the brick, but it felt all wrong. The trajectory was way off. Have you ever done something and then asked God to suspend the laws of physics? Well, God said no. The speed of the car combined with the arch of the rock and yes, you guessed it...the brick hit the windshield and it shattered. The car screeched to a halt.

I did what any six-year-old could think to do—I ran. But not home. I knew better than that. I hid on the far side of the house being demolished, under a tree. I closed my eyes tightly and covered them with my hands because

I thought if I couldn't see you, then you couldn't see me. The driver found me, picked me up by my shirt collar and demanded to know where I lived.

I didn't know the man that had a hold on me, but I knew my father and I knew this would be bad. This man held the back of my shirt collar tightly and it felt like my feet weren't even touching the ground all the way down the street. Finally, we reached my house and he knocked on our screen door, still holding onto me. Dad answered the door, looked at him, looked at me, and asked, "What happened?" Dad told me to come inside and wait in his room. Since six-year-old me didn't have a job, I paid for the new windshield partly with my backside and partly with my allowance. That was the day I stopped throwing rocks over roads.

In life, sometimes we make choices that lead to trouble. We know exactly what we did wrong and why the consequences are what they are. Other times, we are like the man driving along the highway and out of nowhere, things shatter before our eyes. Trouble doesn't make an appointment—it just barges in. That's what our leader Joshua experienced next.

Mountaintops and Deep Valleys

Joshua must have felt on top of the world following the battle of Jericho. He was confident and ready to face the next battle that it appears as if he just launched forward in their battle planning for the city of Ai, without taking much time to consult with the Lord for direction. But we know something Joshua didn't. There was trouble in the camp.

> *"But the Israelites were unfaithful in regard to the devoted things...*
> *So the Lord's anger burned against Israel"* (Joshua 7:1).

Joshua 7 begins on that interesting note. It's a one-sentence introduction that sets the stage for the epic battle and failure that takes place in the Valley of Achor—which not so coincidentally means "trouble." Immediately following this opening revelation, we read that Joshua sends in spies, as he has become accustomed to doing. Their report is positive. The Israelites can easily defeat the men of Ai, and don't need their entire army to do it. So they rush into battle and here's what happens:

> *"So about three thousand went up; but they were routed by the men of Ai, who killed about thirty-six of them. They chased the Israelites from the city gate as far as the stone quarries and struck them down on the slopes. At this the hearts of the people melted in fear and became like water"* (Joshua 7:4-5).

In one fell swoop, the Israelites are caught off guard and suffered a disappointing defeat. Joshua was used to winning. During his time with Moses, Joshua had already fought six major battles and won every one. Joshua's all time win-loss record for battles was 36-1. [5] Ai would be his only loss. While we can learn from our victories, we tend to learn the most from our losses. To describe losing as a shock to Joshua would be like saying, "It's a bit cold today," while standing in the middle of Siberia in the dead of winter. If you've had the wind knocked out of you so that you couldn't breathe, or received such devastating news that you couldn't think straight, you have had a glimpse of what Joshua must have felt.

What is Your First Reaction to Trouble?

Have you ever blown a tire? Ever blown one on the way to work when you were already running late? If we let them, our thoughts become a runaway train headed to Station "D" for despair. "Oh great. I'm gonna be late for work. If I am late for work again, I'm likely to get fired. If I get fired then I can't make the mortgage payment..." and before you know it, you are unable to pay your bills and living on the street, homeless—all from a blown tire.

Because of the defeat, Joshua has now become both fearful and doubtful. He is baffled at this defeat. God had promised victory, hadn't He? God seemed curiously absent. Hadn't He promised that He'd be with Joshua? At that moment, nothing was going as planned and Joshua rattled off question after question to God, filled with emotion and attitude. It's not wrong to ask powerful and direct questions. I think it's a healthy thing to do whenever you don't know something. How can you know if you don't ask? When I was studying this, I have to admit it was like holding up a mirror to myself. I often react like Joshua did when trouble hits my life. I'm guessing Joshua's questions will sound familiar to you too.

Question 1: "Why did You bring us here to destroy us?" (See Joshua 7:7, 9.)

Whenever trouble shows up, we are inclined to believe that the worst will happen. Joshua's question had an accusatory tone and is more of a statement than a question. It probably seemed to Joshua that God was showing His true colors. A common first response to trouble is to blame God, unless there's an obvious explanation otherwise. But even then, we feel almost compelled to blame God. After all, isn't He all-powerful enough to stop any negative consequences?

When we feel afraid, we can get full of ourselves in a hurry, even to the point of questioning God's motives. Ironically we are quick to blame God when things go wrong, but slow to give Him credit when things go right. We believe God can use bad stuff for good— which He does—but that isn't really what's going on here. For a moment, Joshua accused God of wanting to destroy Israel. After all, God promised to be with Joshua, so what happened?

Question 2: What do I do now that Israel has been defeated? (See Joshua 7:8.)

We tend to make trouble bigger than it really is. I think this question had a tone of smugness, "Well, now what?" This is laughable. I understand that no one likes to lose, but really, "Israel had been defeated?" Maybe they were embarrassed, but defeated? Thirty-six men out of thousands were lost. It's true that any loss is a tragedy and should be mourned, but they were clearly not completely defeated or run out of the Promised Land.

Did Joshua really expect that in the promised life, he would never suffer loss? Apparently, yes. Talk about making a mountain out of molehill. But haven't we been guilty of doing the same thing? Isn't it true that we tend to over-think the impact and influence of one negative event or comment? We get tunnel vision so badly that we can't see beyond our one defeat.

Question 3: "What then will You do to protect Your reputation, Your great name?" (See Joshua 7:9.)

When facing trouble, we worry about what others may think. Although I failed mind-reading class I still somehow find myself engaged in a struggle about worrying what other's may or may not be thinking. Did Joshua really believe that somehow this defeat sullied God's reputation with people who didn't believe in Him anyway? In the first place, those who don't respect God already, won't respect God less because Israel lost a battle. Joshua's self-esteem and confidence may have taken a direct hit, but the Canaanite tribes couldn't respect God less than they already did.

God is not in the business of protecting His reputation because He's God—with a spotless and perfect record. We might not always understand His ways, but a failure to understand God's character or motives is not God's failure, but humankind's.

Question 4: If only we had been content to stay on the other side of the Jordan, we would not be in this situation, would we? (See Joshua 7:7.)

This question leads to looking backwards, and asking "What if we would have stayed on the other side? Could we have avoided this?" Whenever trouble shows up, we second-guess our decision to live the promised life. Joshua's statement had a tone of regret, "If only we had been content to stay on the other side of the Jordan...."

> REGRET HAS NO PLACE WHEN WE ARE LIVING THE PROMISED LIFE.

What?! Did that actually come out of his mouth? Of course there would be battles to fight, but he had fought battles in the wilderness before this. Regret has no place when we are living the promised life.

"If only ..." smacks of unmet expectations or shattered dreams. If you say it enough out loud, it will leave you feeling defeated and depressed. Try it:

If only I had a different body...

If only I had more money...

If only I had married someone else...

If only my kids would have...

If only I hadn't eaten that piece of cake...

If only I had saved more money....

If only I had responded differently...somehow.

I think you get the picture. Rather than say, "If only I...", say, "If only God..." While it's true our decisions and actions have consequences, it's also true that God is bigger than all of our mistakes and regrets piled on high.

Question 5: Why have You brought this trouble on us? (See Joshua 7:7, 9.)

Do you ever overspiritualize your pain and confusion by saying that God caused it? Joshua's question had a definite note of blame. He had convinced himself that God caused the trouble he was in. Period. The end. I quit. I'm going to bed. I imagine all of us have moments when we believed God was the author of the trouble we were facing. Maybe God didn't bring Israel all this way just to destroy them, but at the very least, Joshua thought God was responsible for the trouble they were experiencing. But God wasn't the cause of the trouble at all. God had removed Himself from the equation, and that was what Joshua was feeling.

The bottom line is this: Joshua was wrong and sometimes so are we.

If you have never battled and fought through doubt, fear, and questions then you may not be ready for the next thing God has for you to do. Wrestling with doubts and fears is not a sign of weakness, but of strength. It's definitely not fun, but...

God's Epic Answer

What happens next is fantastic. God could have embarrassed Joshua, but He didn't. Joshua was praying hard. He was trying to figure out what comes after defeat. God responded with a firm and stern command, "Stand up!" In other words, "Stop whining!" or "Look at Me when I'm talking to you!" God follows this with His own question, "Why are you down on your face like that?"

> THE PROMISED LIFE IS MORE ABOUT US BEING ON GOD'S SIDE THAN IT IS ABOUT GOD BEING ON OUR SIDE.

At first God's response appears uncaring and borders on hurtful, if not downright insulting. Yet it is by far the most loving response God could have made. It's the truth Joshua needed to hear most. God's question starts to put things into proper perspective. Then God sheds light on the cause of their defeat: "Israel has sinned...I will not be with you."

God didn't cause the defeat. Their disobedience did. Remember the promised life is more about us being on God's side than it is about God being on our side. In those moments when we don't feel close to God, who moved? Sometimes when we don't feel like God is with us, it may be because, like Israel, we have been disobedient, or someone near us has. As Joshua hears the truth about why Israel failed, I think he grieved for his people, but Joshua is developing grit. From the Lord's perspective, trouble always has a purpose and source.

Obedience Matters

God is holy and God is extremely serious about how you live. It is interesting God revealed to Joshua that someone had sinned, but didn't tell him who it was. An investigation had to take place, one that included every tribe and family. I think that was because we learn and grow stronger through the process of figuring things out and being obedient to follow God's promptings.

Ministry was going well for me and for the church. We had just constructed another building on our property because we were continuing to grow. After ten years, I went on a sabbatical to step back and rest as well as research what the next steps should be.

When I returned from my sabbatical, something was missing. One of the weirdest things was that only a couple of people asked me how the sabbatical went. Despite the weirdness that nagged me, from week to week, things were going well. Smooth sailing. There were now two services with six hundred people and new people were being saved every week. But something under the surface was amiss and I couldn't put my finger on it. Have you ever felt like there might be a hole in your boat? You are still afloat and sailing forward, but where is that little bit of water coming from?

Well, the hole in the boat finally revealed itself. One day Beth answered the phone at home. It was one of our elder's wives. "Beth, he told me he doesn't love me anymore. He is going to leave me," the woman said. It blew us both away. We were clueless. This elder was a super nice guy and a very influential leader.

Though I didn't know all the details just yet, I knew this situation could not be ignored. I called the elder and asked to meet the next morning. Before going to bed that night, I prayed fervently for the words God would have me say. What would I say if he was repentant? What should I say if he wasn't? I prayed that God would give me insight. During the night, I woke up, wrote down what God was impressing on me to say to him, and then I slept like a baby. At 6:00 a.m. I was sitting at their house. As he began to share with me that there was another woman, I knew why I couldn't put my finger on the feeling that something was off. It had been hidden from me until now. One of my lead guys was involved in sin...and it was so painful. Part of the strangeness of it all was when he said to me, "Dan, I really hate to do this to you on your watch."

While I hoped and prayed for repentance, the truth is this man never backed down. I had to deliver a stern message from the Lord. It was for him and no one else. I had no malice, but I was straightforward. It was hard, but I said the words God had given me to say. Then, I did my best to shepherd his family through the extremely difficult time ahead.

Sin Exposed

What do you do with sin when it creeps into your camp? Like Joshua, you have to deal with it before you can move forward. We grow stronger through the process of figuring things out. Sometimes we are forced to wrestle to find the answer to a problem and have to dig up the root to the source of a problem. Joshua discovered that Achan, one of his leaders, had taken items from Jericho. These were items they were specifically commanded not to take. Leaders cannot sweep sin under the rug or participate in cover-ups. When Joshua got to the root of the problem, all that was left to do was to remove it. As a lesson to all Israel, they took Achan and his family and killed them. Then they burned the things that had been stolen. Then stones were piled up in that place as a reminder:

> *"Over Achan they heaped up a large pile of rocks, which remains to this day. Then the Lord turned from his fierce anger. Therefore that place has been called the Valley of Achor ever since"* (Joshua 7:26).

Sometimes the consequences are harsh. This is a hard truth for leaders to comprehend at times: Some of the people who started with you are not going to finish with you. Achan was not some guy in the camp. He was someone Joshua knew very well. He was one of the insiders and a selected warrior from the tribe of Judah. Yet what Joshua couldn't know was what Achan hid.

Leaders find it difficult to say this or that must end. But at the end of the day, it is about the holiness of God. In this instance, the clearly stated and understood will of God was being ignored. God was angry.

> SOME OF THE PEOPLE WHO STARTED WITH YOU ARE NOT GOING TO FINISH WITH YOU.

Because Joshua feared God more than the people and wanted to honor God, he took steps to root out the problem.

Of course, stoning doesn't happen today. We live under the covenant of grace. That doesn't mean we don't deal with trouble when it comes our way or when we learn of sin that should be addressed though.

My Agenda – God's Agenda = Failure

God promised military victories in the Promised Land and delivered them in convincing fashion. The only exception, which I mentioned before, is in this battle of Ai. The main thing to note about this incident is that Israel broke faith with God in regards to the "devoted things." God had commanded the Israelites to devote everything to destruction from the battle of Jericho, but Achan had kept some of the loot for himself (See Joshua 6:17). Because of this, God judged them by not giving them the victory at Ai, a much smaller city. These two battle stories, side by side, show that when God sets the agenda, victory follows, but when man sets it, failure ensues. Jericho was the Lord's battle; Ai was not.

God redeemed the situation and eventually gave them the victory, but until then things were bad. The people were understandably discouraged and felt vulnerable to their enemies. Maybe worst of all was that Joshua didn't have a clue how to fix things because he didn't know what the cause of the trouble was. Maybe you've had moments when you've faced trouble and it wasn't because you were careless in making the decision to move forward. Maybe you were convinced that it was God's will for you to do so.

Don't Get Ahead of Yourself...or God

I can't help but wonder how an intuitive leader, like Joshua, didn't realize that God was angry, and that God had removed Himself from them prior to battle. How did Joshua miss that? I wonder what would have happened if Joshua had slowed down and sought the Lord's guidance before marching against Ai. Could things have turned out differently? Achan's sin would still be there, but maybe Joshua would have learned about it before it was too late and more lives were lost.

Joshua 7 does not record any communication or prayer between Joshua and God before sending in the spies, or any mention of the people consecrating themselves like they had in the previous battle. God had given very explicit directions for the battle of Jericho. Joshua might have gotten ahead of himself and God by not giving God the opportunity to lay out the battle plan beforehand. If he had, he may have heard the warning that God was not with them in this one.

Re-examine Your Beliefs about Troubles and Trials

Wrong beliefs can lead to wrong responses when trouble comes. Joshua was shocked with the outcome of the battle against Ai. He may have made the assumption that all the battles would be easy, and the promised life would be without trouble. He had temporary amnesia, forgetting the Lord's commands for him to be very courageous and strong. We don't need courage if there is no battle to fight and no trouble to face.

A common misconception today is that God wants certain things for us that He never promised. It can be too easy to take passages of Scripture out of their original context. Some misinterpreted passages can lead us to expect certain favorable outcomes when God never promised we would be without trouble. For instance: many misapply Jeremiah 29:11, *"'For I know the plans I have for you,' declares the Lord, 'plans to prosper you and not to harm you, plans to give you hope and a future.'"* In context, God was not promising a better immediate future, as we might often hope is the case. The proceeding verse, Jeremiah 29:10 says, *"When seventy years are completed for Babylon...."* In this

> A COMMON MISCONCEPTION TODAY IS THAT GOD WANTS CERTAIN THINGS FOR US THAT HE NEVER PROMISED.

prophecy Jeremiah was bringing hope to God's Old Testament people Israel of a better future, although many of them would never experience it. They were living in exile because they had been defeated, but at least they had hope that God would bring His people back to the Promised Land again. It is a message of hope for a better future, not an immediately easy life. Where are you? Are you in the midst of defeat? Are you living a life impacted by past failure with little hope of immediate change? Quoting that verse out of the original context can be harmful and lead to a loss of hope.

Jesus was the Master at delivering hard truths and hope simultaneously. He said, *"I have told you these things, so that in me you may have peace. In this world you will have trouble. But take heart! I have overcome the world"* (John 16:33). We are not

> GOD'S PLAN FOR YOU IS WONDERFUL, BUT IT IS NOT WITHOUT DIFFICULTY, PAIN, AND HARDSHIP.

promised an easy life, although you might hear that God has a wonderful plan for your life from various preachers. God's plan for you is wonderful, but it is not without difficulty, pain, and hardship.

This wrong belief that we will never experience defeat or heartbreak may explain why some Christians leave the faith. Because many base their decision to follow Christ on having a wonderful life, free from pain and trouble, can lead to a false conversion, followed by a large number that fall away when the going gets tough. While some make following Christ a matter of legalistic perfection, others have reduced following Christ to an easy path rather than a narrow road. We've made Jesus a servant rather than a Master. We want a simple road, a painless cross, and lightweight burdens.

Yet we deal with a plethora of problems on a weekly basis. On the world stage we silently wonder, how do we reconcile this idea of a wonderful life with the large group of Christians massacred in Africa? Or closer to home, what do you tell the Christian family who lost their child in the prime of his or her life? Or the young woman who receives the diagnosis that she has an advanced form of cancer? How do I reconcile my father's death at sixty-four after living a life of dedicated service to the Lord? How do we make sense of the disciples? Eleven of the twelve were martyred.

What if promotional material for one of America's elite Special Forces such as the Green Berets, Delta Force or Navy Seals read, "Limited time to be stationed in numerous exotic locations. All training, exciting excursions and travel associated with your work will be paid for by Uncle Sam." Anyone who joined would be immediately disillusioned and disappointed because they were not told the whole truth about what was involved. This is the result when we fail to tell the whole truth as Christ did. *"I have told you these things, so that in me you may have peace. In this world you will have trouble. But take heart! I have overcome the world!"* (John 16:33). In view of eternity, there is hope for today.

The Right Belief about Trouble

Begin with the solid belief that God is good. Everything hinges on who He is. Train your thoughts and heart to be convinced of His love for you and trust Him. He is your peace when you feel anxious or afraid, or when you wrestle through unanswered prayers, trouble, bad news, or hardship. Because you have a new set point you can then be confident in your actions. The fact you are in a storm doesn't change the truth that God is good and that He is with you; you experience a deep inner peace even at these times, not because you ignore the reality of the storm, but because you are aware of God's presence. You are secure in His eternal plan. Leaders, we are greatly remiss if we fail to teach this balance.

Anchors work, even during a storm, because they rest in the deep water where there is calm. Your faith is secured in who God is, so troublesome times don't break us apart. Trying times are not intended to crush you, but build your character instead. How else can we build qualities, such as love, joy, patience, kindness, faithfulness, and self-control except to be confronted with situations that

> THE FACT YOU ARE IN A STORM DOESN'T CHANGE THE TRUTH THAT GOD IS GOOD AND THAT HE IS WITH YOU; YOU EXPERIENCE A DEEP INNER PEACE EVEN AT THESE TIMES, NOT BECAUSE YOU IGNORE THE REALITY OF THE STORM, BUT BECAUSE YOU ARE AWARE OF GOD'S PRESENCE.

require those qualities? Even Christ *"...learned obedience from what he suffered"* (Heb. 5:8). Patience develops as we are tested. Love is shaped when we choose to love those who do not love us. Forgiveness is learned only when we feel wronged. Faithfulness to God is tested when we feel like we are losing. Joy increases as we focus our thoughts on the goodness of God, especially in the midst of difficult times.

God does bless His people, and He desires that we enjoy His blessings (See 1 Tim. 6:17-19). But a wonderful, comfortable life is not what we should pursue. Instead we should pursue the presence of God. Psalm 29:11 says, *"The Lord gives strength to his people; the Lord blesses his people with peace."* Strength in the face of adversity is a true blessing. Paul's great motto for life was, *"...I have learned to be content whatever the circumstances"* (Phil. 4:11b).

Disregarding God's Direction

Let's talk for a moment about sin, because that is where the trouble all started: Achan's sin. What is sin? The definition of sin borrows its definition from the Greek world. The Greek word is *harmatia* which is a term used by archers. The goal of an archer was to shoot the bullseye on a target. If the archer missed the bullseye, then he committed *harmatia* meaning that he missed the target. Biblically, sin is when we miss the mark.

One target is when God says *not to do* something. If I do that thing anyway, I have missed the mark. In the case of Israel, Achan had sinned by doing what God commanded them not to do. This is sometimes called a sin of commission because it's something I choose to do, even though God said not to do that thing. When Adam and Eve ate fruit from the Tree of the Knowledge of Good and Evil that was considered a sin of commission because God had commanded them not to eat from that tree. If God says don't and we do, we've missed the mark.

Another type of target is one in which God commands us *to do* something and we choose not to do that thing. For example, God commands us to love our neighbor as we love ourselves. On those occasions in which I choose to *not* love my neighbor, I have missed the mark. I have committed *harmatia*. This is sometimes called a sin of omission because I chose to ignore a clear command from God.

Another target for us is to live by *your* faithfulness to God and His people in matters of opinion. In matters of opinion, the question is not whether something is right or wrong, but the impact your decision or action may have on the faith of those around you. For example, your faith may allow you to drive an expensive car, or participate in Halloween, but is it beneficial to those around you? Just because you can doesn't mean you should. Are you doing this or buying that because you believe it will glorify God? If so, then that means you are acting according to your faith. Paul said, *"...whatever does not proceed from faith is sin"* (Rom. 14:23, ESV). Your faith may allow you to do those things, but is it beneficial to those around you? Again, just because you can doesn't mean you should. Will my actions cause those who follow me to do the same even though they may not do it by faith? Leaders must be conscious of the fact that they have a responsibility towards God's people to lead them well. The lifestyle choices we make have an impact on others. It is a wrong to disregard the influence you have on others around you.

JUST BECAUSE YOU CAN DOESN'T MEAN YOU SHOULD.

When We Bring Trouble upon Ourselves

Achan had missed the mark big time and everyone was about to figure that out. But had you been in the Israelite camp, you may not have looked at Achan as a likely suspect. He was involved and trusted. He was also a hypocrite because he pretended that all was well when it was not. How does someone end up in such deep trouble?

While this book is about learning leadership lessons from Joshua, there are leadership lessons we can learn from Achan as well— hard lessons. First, don't name your child Achan. You're asking for trouble because the name literally meant troubler. In all seriousness though, some of the best lessons we learn in life are from bad examples, not good ones.

As mentioned earlier, Achan wasn't just any guy in the camp. He was from the tribe of Judah. He was probably one of the 40,000 warriors to first cross the Jordan. He had been at Jericho. He was one of the 3,000 warriors chosen to defeat Ai. If Joshua was King Arthur, Achan would have been one of the knights at his round table. Achan knew what it was like to be on top of things. He had heard how God rescued his parents and grandparents from Egypt. He knew of the plagues and he'd probably listened a hundred times about how his ancestors walked through the Red Sea on dry ground. He also knew about how his parents had been faithless and how God had miraculously fed and clothed the people for forty years. But for some reason he thought he could ignore God's clear direction and get away with it.

The strength of Achan's body was no match for the strength of his desires. Who hasn't walked this path? He won the battle on the outside impressively, yet lost the battle within miserably. It was a battle between obedience versus self-interest. Let's be honest, sometimes we are like Achan. We see, we want, we take, we hide.

I have wondered as all the tribes were being assembled and then each father in the family from the tribe was brought forth, what was going through Achan's mind? Achan lacked the courage to step up and confess his sin. Yes, he did tell the truth when asked. We don't know what was going on, but evidently something on Achan's face or in his demeanor led Joshua to confront him directly. Joshua said, *"Tell me what you have done; do not hide it from me."* (Josh. 7:19).

I can imagine Achan had practiced his speech while he was waiting in a long line to face Joshua. *"Achan replied, 'It is true! I have sinned against the Lord, the God of Israel. This is what I have done: When I saw in the plunder a beautiful robe from Babylonia, two hundred shekels of silver and a bar of gold weighing fifty shekels, I coveted them and took them. They are hidden in the ground inside my tent, with the silver underneath'"* (Josh. 7:20-21).

The Anatomy of Temptation

James 1:14-15 says, *"...but each person is tempted when they are dragged away by their own evil desire and enticed. Then, after desire has conceived, it gives birth to sin; and sin, when it is full-grown, gives birth to death."* This perfectly describes Achan's quick journey from a faithful leader to the grave. When he is found out, Achan goes through a step-by-step explanation almost as if wanting to justify himself. What was going through his mind? Did he think: *Maybe if I walk through this slowly and explain HOW I got here and WHY I did it... maybe it won't seem so awful. Maybe it will seem like less of a big deal.* So Achan described the four steps: He saw something he wanted, he coveted what he wanted, he took what he wanted, and finally he hid what he wanted. Let's take a closer look at the anatomy of temptation.

"I saw." Achan saw some stuff he wanted. It's not necessarily a sin to see something. It's what we do next that matters more. Maybe he thought it would improve his life. The bottom line is that he wanted what he saw. That's how Achan described it next.

"I coveted." Coveting is wanting something that is not ours. While most sin is obvious to an observer, coveting is not at all obvious to others. It can be masked and hidden instead. We can give the appearance of perfect obedience when in truth, we are filled with a desire for what we do not and should not have. Rather than focusing on obedience to God, Achan coveted what he saw and in that moment, he lost focus.

"I took." We take things because we want them. We steal because we think that we'll get away with it. Achan took what he wanted. He was one of thousands in the nation of Israel. Surely no one would notice. And, anyway, was it really stealing? The people who used to own it were dead. What Achan forgot was that everything in Jericho was devoted as firstfruits to the Lord. Someone else already did own it.

"I hid." Really, if you must hide something is it worth having? Apparently, yes. Why did he hide it? Because he knew that he wasn't supposed to have it. Probably like us at times, he thought that no one would know. But God knew, Achan knew, and his family knew too.

Operation Cover-Up

When we hide something, we begin living as an agent of Operation Cover-up. Hiding something when we know we shouldn't have it in the first place is like holding a ticking time bomb. We know that someday it will explode. We just don't know when. That thing we so badly wanted is now destroying us. Desire something long enough and you may just get it.

Achan got what he wanted, but then had to hide it. He couldn't enjoy it. He hid it because he knew he wasn't supposed to have it. It's one thing to do something wrong because you're clueless or dumb. It's quite another thing to be so calculated. Is the thrill of knowing you have it more important than doing the right thing? And do you have it or at that point does it have you?

The thing that Achan thought would make him rich made him poor. The moment Achan took hold of the robe and the silver is the same moment it took hold of him. When he returned to camp he lived to protect that stuff. How many of us live to protect stuff rather than living "all out"? The thing that he thought might improve his life, in fact destroyed his life. Integrity? Gone. Restful sleep? Gone. It's true for us as well. Sometimes, the thing that we think might improve our life ends up being the thing that destroys us.

But there is another way. You don't have to continue living as an undercover agent. No matter where you are on the path towards death, you can get off it and experience life.

Faking Cancer

A woman in our church asked to speak with me and I could tell it was a sensitive situation. She began one day, "You know, Shannon in our congregation keeps asking for prayers for her cancer and she says she is going through treatment. Dan, as a woman who is battling cancer currently myself, I don't think she has cancer. Her behavior doesn't match what she is asking the church to pray for." People had also given Shannon money and tried to help her out. This was certainly a strange situation. I'm usually optimistic and want to think the best of people. The more I thought and prayed about the situation though, the stronger the prompting of the Holy Spirit was to confront Shannon about her diagnosis.

"Shannon, we need to talk," I said over the phone a few days later.

At first she declined, "No I don't want to talk about this. It's very personal."

I persisted and said, "No, I think we really do need to talk." I also asked her to bring some medical records.

Then she said, "Okay, well, can I bring some friends with me?"

"Sure, you can bring anyone you want," I replied.

On the evening we met, Shannon brought four other people with her for support.

It was awkward, but I knew I needed to get right to the point. "We love you and want to help in any way we can through this difficult time, but Shannon, your behavior doesn't match what you are telling us. It is taking a lot of energy and time from people who love you very much. Is there anything you want to tell us?" I asked.

"No," she answered, and proceeded to stick to her story about cancer.

I finally said, "I don't believe you have cancer."

She went on to tell three or four different stories. With each of the stories, the spirit inside me said to confront her, that she was not telling the truth. Each time I did, she backed down and changed her story. Until finally, she relented. It was, in fact, all made up. She just wanted attention. Everyone in the room was shocked and Shannon was embarrassed.

Are you forming the habits necessary to hear from the Spirit and have the courage to act on His promptings? I'll be the first to admit that I don't always get it right. Most of the time though, as leaders, we do know the truth. The Spirit has laid it upon us. What we really lack is the courage to confront and ask for the truth with grace.

Shannon wanted to go to another church. With as much grace and truth as I could grasp, I told her that was a bad idea. I remember her reply clearly.

"Don't I deserve a fresh start?"

"Oh yes! You do deserve that, but with your ability and giftedness at lying, you need to be around people that know you and love and will give you a true fresh start," I said.

Defeat Can Lead to Success

We must face trouble head on, like Joshua did. Maybe you are in a season of that right now and you need to hear God saying to you, "Stand up! Why are you down on your face?" We all need to hear that from time to time. Get up out of your indecision, misery, bitterness, or cynicism and find out where the trouble is really coming from: whether it is within yourself or within your team. Leaders take responsibility for themselves and the people they are leading. They are tasked with uncovering truth and cutting through self-deception. Ask God to reveal what you need to know, when you need to know it, and have the courage to investigate, like Joshua did.

> LEADERS TAKE RESPONSIBILITY FOR THEMSELVES AND THE PEOPLE THEY ARE LEADING. THEY ARE TASKED WITH UNCOVERING TRUTH AND CUTTING THROUGH SELF-DECEPTION.

Defeat leads to success when you learn from it and take action and do something new. These painful experiences are used by God to open the doors of victory. The turning point in my situation was made possible through repentance and dependence on the Lord. The same was true for Joshua. The place which marked defeat became the passage to something new and great. Through this door, Israel was sent back to war and instead of defeat, there was victory. Don't be afraid of failing. Be more afraid of not knowing the real reason behind the failure. Those who do not learn from their mistakes are doomed to repeat them.

I had the privilege of meeting the former football quarterback and baseball outfielder, Tim Tebow, one weekend at our church. That's one guy who knows a lot about winning and losing. We hosted him as guest speaker and I got to spend a few minutes with him. We talked about some of our high points and low points. He said: "People don't relate to your highs. But everyone can relate to your lows...low points, and failures." Isn't that true. The writer of Hebrews says, *"Endure hardship as discipline; God is treating you as his children. For what children are not disciplined by their father?"* (Heb. 12:7). Losing battles and overcoming trouble causes us to draw nearer to God and nearer to others.

Hebrews 4:15-16, ESV, says, *"Since then we have a great high priest who has passed through the heavens, Jesus, the Son of God, let us hold fast our confession. For we do not have a high priest who is unable to sympathize with our weaknesses, but one who in every respect has been tempted as we are, yet without sin. Let us then with confidence draw near to the throne of grace, that we may receive mercy and find grace to help in time of need."*

Listen and Take a Lesson from the Dead

In the movie *Remember the Titans,* it's three in the morning and coach Herman Boone, played by Denzel Washington, wakes up his high school football team during training camp. "We're gonna take a little run through the woods," he tells the young players.

They run through the woods, into a creek, and across a stone footbridge. As the sun is peaking through the trees, the exhausted team stops at their destination. They are now standing on the edge of a burial ground, where the battle of Gettysburg was fought.

"Fifty thousand men died right here, fighting the same fight we are still fighting today...," says Coach Boone. "Listen to their souls, men...Listen and take a lesson from the dead. If we don't come together right now on this hallowed ground, we too, will be destroyed."

Like the monuments at Gettysburg, the pile of stones built on the family of Achan served as a reminder for the Israelites that obedience matters. This memorial between the people and God was a sobering one. It is a lesson for us today as well. We cannot hide from God and He cannot be present with us in our disobedience. Winning external battles depends greatly on winning the internal battles first. While Joshua battled his doubts, Achan battled his desires. Joshua turned to God in his battle with doubt. Achan buried his sin and it buried him.

Beliefs >> Thoughts >> Actions >> Habits >> Character >> Destiny

Do you see how Achan's **disbelief** in God led to **thoughts** of coveting, and then the **action** of stealing? After this, a **habit** of hiding began, tarnishing his **character,** which ultimately led to a fateful **destiny.**

Obedience matters.

Chapter 5

MONUMENT THREE: GET BACK UP!

"So do not throw away your confidence...you need to persevere..."
—Hebrews 10:35-36a

When the Dust Clears

COMEBACKS. WE LOVE a good comeback story, don't we? Whether it is the Cubs winning Game 7 of the World Series in 10 innings or the surfer who gets back on the board after being attacked by a shark...comebacks are the best. At least they are after the fact. It's not so fun when you are in the middle of them though.

When I was thirteen I loved dirt biking. Once I was out in the desert, riding with six other guys. They were older and had bigger, faster motorcycles than me, so I spent most of my time eating their dust. Then came my opportunity to pass them. They were slowing down, so I sped up to over fifty miles per hour. My plan was to rush through them even though I couldn't see through the dust cloud. At the same moment I cleared the dust, everything became clear as to the reason they had slowed down. There were dirt mounds and valleys created by the wind everywhere, but it was too late for me to stop.

What happened next is still burned into my memory. My thought going into it was, *Hey I'm going to get ahead.* Then time seemed to slow to one millisecond at a time as everyone watched me hit every bump until finally crashing into the dirt. I had the breath knocked out of me and one of the guys told me, "The best way to get out of here is to get back on your bike and ride out. But if you can't, we will find another way."

My comeback wasn't that I won that race through the desert, but that I got back on the bike. Sometimes when we crash, we give up. Those guys did me a huge favor, advising me to get right back on the bike, so I would not fear riding in the future. After catching my breath and a minute of rest, I rode out of the desert and continued riding even into adulthood. They praised me for getting back on and riding the motorcycle out. That incident has served as a metaphor for other moments in my life when I had to catch my breath and keep going.

For there to be a comeback there has to be failure or at least a falling behind. Our God is a huge fan of comebacks too! In fact, He is the ultimate Storyteller and Creator of comebacks. Joshua and the Israelites are about to have one in this next monumental moment.

Hitting Rock Bottom

Let's pick up where we left off. So there lies Achan and his family, under a pile of stones. Now what? Understanding and addressing what caused the defeat in the first battle of Ai was necessary, but it didn't remove the feelings of discouragement, shame or grief over what happened. In addition to the burial site of Achan's family, there were also thirty-six other graves to be dug for the men lost in that battle.

Have you ever been in the aftermath of a disaster or defeat? Maybe you are like Joshua, and you lost a good man or woman from your team because of sin. Maybe you are a little like Achan: You aren't dead underneath a pile of stones but you feel the weight of your sin or shame still crushing you, and holding you down. Suffering defeat can be exhausting. Enough so that

> ROCK BOTTOM CAN BECOME THE SOLID FOUNDATION UPON WHICH TO BUILD AGAIN.

you want to give up. Joshua 7 ends with a sense of hitting rock bottom—a literal pile of rocks. Rock bottom can become the solid foundation upon which to build again.

Re-examine Your Beliefs about Failure and Pain

"If at first you don't succeed, try, try again." We've probably all heard that famous maxim and if you are a parent, you have probably said that to your children as they learned to ride a bike, tied their shoes, didn't make the team, or get into their first choice of college. We encourage others to get back up and try again, but do we really believe that failure isn't final at the very core of our own beings? It's easier said than done.

Discouragement following a failure or painful circumstance can cause us to vacillate, meaning we waver on taking any next steps forward. Feelings of discouragement damage our confidence and strip us of courage. The quickest way to get discouraged and disillusioned is to look at people and circumstances as the determining factors in your life.

> THE QUICKEST WAY TO GET DISCOURAGED AND DISILLUSIONED IS TO LOOK AT PEOPLE AND CIRCUMSTANCES AS THE DETERMINING FACTORS IN YOUR LIFE.

The truth is that people will fail you and circumstances will falter. You can depend on that. I think that is why God's first words to Joshua after creating the monument of Achan were both an encouragement and a realignment to the promise of victory.

> "...Do not be afraid; do not be discouraged. Take the whole army with you, and go up and attack Ai. For I have delivered into your hands the king of Ai, his people, his city and his land. You shall do to Ai and its king as you did to Jericho and its king, except that you may carry off their plunder and livestock for yourselves. Set an ambush behind the city" (Joshua 8:1-2).

God was with them. God still had a plan for Israel and He would be victorious. If we choose to believe that failure and pain are opportunities to learn, then failure and pain take on a whole new meaning. They have purpose.

Monumental leaders look back over life realistically only to discover that painful moments became doors of hope and greater dependence on God. Pain gives us the opportunity to practice perseverance. Failure is never final for the one who learns to persevere.

Developing Perseverance

Perseverance is steadfastness. It is doing something despite difficulty or delay in achieving success. And that's exactly what Joshua experienced—a delay to success. He never gave up, although if anyone could have given up, it was Joshua. For most of his life, he was living among a bunch of loser-faithless-type people. He suffered because of what others had done. Wouldn't you have understood had he chosen to give up? I know

> IF WE CHOOSE TO BELIEVE THAT FAILURE AND PAIN ARE OPPORTUNITIES TO LEARN, THEN FAILURE AND PAIN TAKE ON A WHOLE NEW MEANING. THEY HAVE PURPOSE.

I would have. However, Joshua had learned how to consistently and faithfully cooperate with God. He did not allow losses to freeze him in place or develop an attitude against the Lord or the Lord's people.

Regardless what path you choose to walk in life, failure and setbacks will occur. Some of these things will be brought on by others; some will be self-induced. You can do everything right and still have something bad happen. While the desire not to fail is admirable, perfection can be a dangerous and destructive illusion. Perseverance is developing resolve to serve God, regardless of the outcomes. While circumstances change, God's Word and His promises never do.

Monumental leaders must develop perseverance, especially following failure. Scripture declares that God uses suffering to train His children, much like a father does for his children. But sometimes, as troubles, failures, or pain pile up, the desire to just call it quits is overwhelming. Confidence to take another step seems far out of reach. Almost every leader we read about in the Scriptures had a moment when they were ready to give up.

Don't Throw Away Your Confidence

Like Joshua, the New Testament Christians had their share of defeating situations. They were at risk of losing their confidence because, in addition to great persecution from those outside the church, they were under pressure from individuals known as Judaizers—fellow Christians who insisted that in addition to following Jesus Christ, everyone should also follow the Law of Moses. I think that we can all understand the pressure when those around us become legalistic in their approach and application of Scripture. In the midst of suffering, the writer of Hebrews offers this encouragement and promise:

> *"So do not throw away your confidence; it will be richly rewarded"*
> (Hebrews 10:35).

This is an encouragement, a command with a promise, much like the Lord's words to Joshua. How can we keep our confidence? Hebrews 10 outlines the actions and attitudes we can take to keep our confidence and develop perseverance.

1) **Remember the source of your confidence is Jesus.** *"Therefore, brothers and sisters, since we have confidence to enter the Most Holy Place by the blood of Jesus, by a new and living way opened for us through the curtain, that is, his body, and since we have a great priest over the house of God"* (Heb. 10:19-21).

2) **Be genuine in your relationship with God.** *"...let us draw near to God with a sincere heart and with the full assurance that faith brings..."* (Heb. 10:22a).

3) **Confess and start fresh.** *"...having our hearts sprinkled to cleanse us from a guilty conscience and having our bodies washed with pure water"* (Heb. 10:22b).

4) **Let hope lead the way.** *"Let us hold unswervingly to the hope we profess, for he who promised is faithful"* (Heb. 10:23).

5) **Don't play it safe. It will destroy you.** *"But we do not belong to those who shrink back and are destroyed..."* (Heb. 10:39a).

6) **Walk in faith and really live!** *"...but to those who have faith and are saved"* (Heb. 10:39b).

All of us will face situations in which we feel like giving up and throwing in the towel, just like Joshua and the first century Christians we just read about in Hebrews. Not all challenges are the same and not everyone suffers the same challenges. However, it is

> TRIALS PRODUCE PEOPLE WITH SPIRITUAL STAMINA.

remarkable that Christianity produces individuals who, rather than shrink away, respond to the challenges such as slander, threats, abuse, and injury with forgiveness. God created His people, each one, with the capability to respond like Christ to these difficult, hurtful, and sometimes horrific situations. It's not that we always respond to every circumstance all the time in ways that reflect the grace of God in our lives. It's that we are capable of responding to everything in a way that reflects our faith in God.

Trials produce people with spiritual stamina. Why is this true? Because Christ's death produces people *"who are being made holy"* (Heb. 10:14). That's why Christians were encouraged not to throw away their confidence. Well-placed confidence may be one of the most valuable characteristics we have. I'm not talking about confidence for the sake of confidence, but rather confidence in Christ's power to save.

Swept Away

What can happen when we do throw our confidence away? We can lose our ability to move forward. This happened to Velentina, a woman of great insight and faith who attended services where I preached. She had been listening to my sermons about Joshua and Caleb and how they were hopeful, confident and optimistic about the future because they believed God. Hope does not come easy, yet Joshua and Caleb chose to believe God and follow Him wholeheartedly. She sent me an e-mail and her story is a perfect example of what it looks like for a follower of Christ to lose confidence and hope and then gain it again. Here it is: [6]

Hello Dan,

This is Velentina. I want to share with you what God is doing in my life. I hope this encourages you. Six years ago, while I was eight months pregnant with my second child, I discovered that my mother had been swept away in a flash flood. She lived in Puerto Rico and the hurricane season brought increased rain. I spoke with her on a Monday for three hours and the next day after work she was tossed into a river on her way to town. Dan, her death was horrific. People stood by as they helplessly saw my mother crying and reaching out for help from the hood of her car. Another crash of water came and they found her body twenty miles down the river about forty-eight hours later.

Something happened to my faith that day. I didn't think it affected my faith, but it did. Having been a Christian for over ten years at that point, I knew better than to "blame God" or even ask "why." I was grateful that my mother had returned to God and I know she will live in eternity. What did happen was that I lost hope. My childlike, innocent faith that I had was gone.

Today, six years later, I cried all the way to work as God revealed to me that I stopped believing in Him to heal, to work, and to transform. I told a friend that I used to believe those Scriptures about believing that anything could happen if we just have the faith of a mustard seed, but now I believe we should just pray for His will. My friend steadily answered, "Yes this is true but perhaps that thinking keeps one from believing the impossible."

Later that day you preached about having the faith of Caleb who didn't focus on the giants but on God's promises.

You see, I had become very cynical after my mother's death and sneered inwardly when I heard people praying for healing and joy. Didn't they know that we aren't supposed to be happy here on earth? Didn't they understand that our hope is in heaven and that our life here is supposed to be miserable?

I am being healed inwardly as I write this e-mail to you. I know that God has so much for me in this life and in the next, if I will only let Him carry out His purpose for me, if I will follow Him wholeheartedly...if I want to be healed. He is speaking to me about pressing and pushing through like the woman with the blood flow that did not give up and sought to only touch the hem of His garment.

My mother was the first in her generation of our family to know the living God. I am the second and Satan had been subtly working his way into convincing me that hope in Jesus is futile. I had become numb and "asleep" for six years. I got to the point where I no longer shared my faith with others because I didn't know what to tell them anymore. It reflected what was inside of me. I kept saying that it was no use to pray to God for specific requests since His will would prevail, no matter what. I felt defeated.

God is revealing to me how so much of my life scared me and all I was doing was awaiting a day that I might be swept away like my mother. I have focused on all the times that suffering occurred to the believers, without realizing how powerful the joy and peace was that accompanied them. I've glossed over the times that Jesus did heal, restore, or change the course of events because of those who interceded and sought Him with all of their hearts. I believe that God is bringing perspective into my life and restoring faith that once was there. Thank you for your words that are bringing me back to a place of childlike faith. Truly, anything is possible with God.

Respectfully,
Valentina

Wake Up!

Look around and you likely can think of someone who has become numb or asleep in their life. Maybe you know someone who is going through the motions of breathing oxygen and doing what comes next on their to-do list. Maybe that describes you. It is possible to find ourselves living day-to-day without a vibrant and living faith.

Biblically, God desires for every person to live by faith. Most Christ-followers would agree that we are saved by faith. But what about living by faith? What does it mean to live by faith in God? Paul shares what was possibly an early Christian hymn, *"...Wake up, sleeper, rise from the dead, and Christ will shine on you"* (Eph. 5:14).

Paul also says the power of the gospel lies in the fact that through the gospel we learn of a righteousness that is from God. He writes: *"...from faith for faith, as it is written, 'The righteous shall live by faith'"* (Rom. 1:17b, ESV).

While we are indeed saved by faith, we are also called to live by faith. The idea of being saved by faith is slightly more tangible than the concept of living by faith. I wonder how many know about the saving faith of Christ, but are asleep to living by faith, like Valentina was? Trusting in Jesus Christ to save me is one thing, but trusting Him in all things in life is quite another.

When Israel had been safely delivered out of Egypt, there was no reason to cross the Jordan River. When they were safely out of Egypt, one might wonder why it was necessary to travel farther. What's more, God was with them. They could see the pillar of fire and the cloud. He provided manna to eat and water to drink. Why bother moving forward? God didn't want to just save them; He wanted them to live abundantly by faith.

Why would someone today not live abundantly? It may be because living by faith requires that we engage fully in our relationships, our attitudes, our emotions, and our intellect. It is one thing for a believer to understand that his identification with Jesus Christ means that he has died to sin (See Romans 6:2) and to believe that to be true (See Romans 6:11). But it is something else entirely for that same person to deal with the sin nature that remains within them as well as its efforts to express itself in their thoughts and actions. This is the internal conflict in the area of sanctification that every believer faces. And this is precisely what this book is about. The story of Joshua is useful for helping us live fully, especially when we hit rock bottom. Monumental leaders point people to a living faith as well as a saving faith.

Richly Rewarded in a Fruitful Valley Called "Trouble"

Now let's travel back to our mentor Joshua and this valley the Israelites are in, both figuratively and literally. The Valley of Achor meant trouble. The phrase "the valley of Achor," became proverbial among the Israelites for anything that caused trouble, calamity, misfortune, or suffering. It was very similar to the phrase we use today when we say, "Don't let this become your Waterloo." Without explanation, you probably know that I'm referring to the Battle of

Waterloo of 1815 in which Napoleon Bonaparte, the French military and political leader, suffered his final defeat.

There is something interesting to note about this Valley of Achor.
Approximately 650 years later the prophet Hosea says the Valley of Achor, which
means "trouble or disaster," will become
a *"door of hope"* (Hosea 2:15). His point
is that God is in the business of turning
disaster into hope and victory. He works
all things together *"for the good of those
who love him, who have been called according to his purpose"* (Rom. 8:28). Maybe
the turnaround doesn't happen immediately but God never wastes a hardship.
He never misses an opportunity to help His people mature.

> GOD IS IN THE BUSINESS OF
> TURNING DISASTER INTO
> HOPE AND VICTORY.

For Joshua, dealing with trouble in the Valley of Achor was the starting
point for greater things that the Lord wanted to do through him. It was not the
end or simply an experiment in trusting God. An important question both then
and now is whether or not we will persevere in faith or vacillate in fear. Do you
realize that God can turn trouble into hope?

Hindsight is 20/20. As we live the promised life, we're able to look back and
discover that times of trouble or pain became doors of hope. Like Joshua at the
place where he faced alarming trouble, it became the spot where his faith and
hope were renewed. Whatever has caused you misfortune or tragedy, can also
become the source of great joy and hope. Give it time, then look back.

"Trouble" and "hope" can be two sides of the same door. The place that
marked defeat became the passage to something new and great. Through this
door, Israel was sent back to war and instead of defeat, there was victory. The
turning point was made possible through repentance and dependence on the
Lord and by not giving discouragement a foothold. I like the way Bob Goff said
it in a 2017 Facebook post, "Fear gives us a reason not to try; hope gives us the
courage not to listen."

If you believe that failure isn't final—because God's grace really is as powerful as Christ promised it would be—then our thoughts about failure can

dramatically change. We need not be stuck in it. Instead we can see failure as an opportunity for growth and change.

New Life Requires New Strategy

After telling Joshua to choose a new attitude, God gave Joshua a new plan, telling him to *"...take the whole army with you...."* (Josh. 8:1a). Joshua needed to do more than just toughen up and persevere; he needed a new strategy. The first time they attacked Ai, they only sent 3,000 warriors to attack the city. This time they were armed with a new attitude and a new strategy—and 30,000 men. Sometimes, we need to learn a new way to live by listening to God's strategy instead of our own.

God promised Joshua success, but he still had to fight the battle. Then God said: "I have delivered them into your hands." Here's where it's easy to go wrong. It's all too easy to sit around waiting on God, or somebody else, to change something in our world. Life doesn't come with a remote. If you don't like what's playing, get up and change the channel yourself. Arm yourself with a new attitude of confidence and a new clear strategy, and get to work. We've all heard: plan the work, and work the plan. Success is promised; effort is required.

As a leader, you will be defined by your ability to take action and inspire others to do the same. While God gives us life, some assembly is required. Israel had to use their minds and might to do what they could to put the new strategy into action. Joshua learned a tough lesson: When God said he would need to be strong, courageous, and obedient, He meant it.

Joshua, with newfound confidence, took the Lord's instruction to send the 30,000 men and set an ambush behind the city. Joshua further assembled the plan by sending men out at night with explicit instructions. His inspiring pre-battle speech:

> *"So Joshua and the whole army moved out to attack Ai. He chose*
> *thirty thousand of his best fighting men and sent them out at*

*night with these orders: 'Listen carefully. You are to set an ambush behind the city. Don't go very far from it. All of you be on the alert. I and all those with me will advance on the city, and when the men come out against us, as they did before, we will flee from them. They will pursue us until we have lured them away from the city, for they will say, "They are running away from us as they did before." So when we flee from them, you are to rise up from ambush and take the city. The **Lord** your God will give it into your hand. When you have taken the city, set it on fire. Do what the **Lord** has commanded. See to it; you have my orders.' Then Joshua sent them off, and they went to the place of ambush and lay in wait between Bethel and Ai, to the west of Ai—but Joshua spent that night with the people"* (Joshua 8:3-9, emphasis mine).*

"See to it. You have my orders." Don't you love the confidence heard in those words? We have Joshua back in the saddle, moving from a questioning leader to a confident one again. His confidence wasn't in himself. He had lost that. Joshua replaced his confidence with confidence in the Lord. *"The Lord your God will give it into your hand."*

Note how Joshua leads the people back to confidence as well. He tells them to *"listen carefully"* and *"be on the alert."* If you have lost your confidence, do the same. Remove distractions. Get to a place where you are focused on listening and learning what God has for you. Listen for His next steps and remember the victory is the Lord's.

After regaining their confidence and following the new plan, Israel won the battle at Ai in good fashion.

Never Stop Flying the Plane

Have you ever had a moment that seemed like a reversal of destiny? One minute everything is going well; then it's not. I'm sure that the sin of Achor and the first battle of Ai felt like that for Joshua. I'll never forget a moment when my friends and I felt like we were in for a reversal of destiny.

I had flown on a friend's plane, along with three others from our church's leadership team, to meet with another church's leadership team in Texas. We were on our final approach at Meacham International Airport in Fort Worth, Texas, when we requested permission to land. We heard back from the tower: "November Four One Four Juliet Sierra, you are cleared for landing." (N414JS was the tail sign on our plane.) The squawking sound was from the control tower and it was business as usual.

As preparations were made for landing, a switch was flipped to open the landing gear. When the switch is turned on, the pilot waits to see three green lights, each in turn, indicating that all three wheels are down and in the locked position. The pilot counted, "one, two..." Then nothing. There were only two green lights, indicating the front and right wheels were locked in. Our third wheel, the left, had not locked in so the green light was not lit. The pilot gently tapped the light to see if maybe it was just a defective connection. Nothing.

To be sure that the landing gear was indeed not in the proper position, we requested a flyby so traffic control could take a look at our landing gear. After two flybys they confirmed that the wheel was not completely down and locked as it should be.

Facing an inevitable landing with the clock running, we tried everything we could while in the air. During this time, the control tower declared an emergency and later informed us they had diverted all air traffic to other airfields nearby so they could focus on helping us land safely. Gathering the facts of the situation, the control tower called again, "Juliet Sierra, how much fuel and how many souls on board?" Our pilot, Joe, calmly responded, "We have four souls on board and enough fuel for two hours." I couldn't help but notice Joe's matter-of-fact demeanor in contrast to the weight of the moment.

Finally, the tower asked Joe, "What are your intentions?" It is protocol in flying that the pilot is in charge and required to make decisions, especially in an emergency. It was time for a decision because we were facing the inevitable:

we would end up on the ground eventually. The only question was how to get there. Joe was forced to make a decision, not because we couldn't stay in the air for a couple more hours, but because inevitably we'd need to land that plane.

Vacillating Could Wreck Your Plan(e)

Have you ever needed a reversal of destiny? You who are faced with an illness...your family is struggling or worse, is breaking apart... financially you're going from bad to worse.... and in some ways God seems absent. You know He isn't, but there are moments when it feels that way. You are wondering how tomorrow will turn out. Times of pain, fear, defeat, grief, and doubt can leave us hopelessly stuck in sadness, loneliness, or misunderstood, and living tentatively. Even during these times God is still at work. Hebrews 13:5 says *"I will never leave you, nor forsake you."* I am convinced that when God seems distant, He is still at work. It is God who works through all the seemingly insignificant coincidences that make up your life, bringing them together for your good. But there are moments when we are forced to make decisions in the middle of painful and troubling circumstances. If we don't persevere—if we don't take a step—if we don't make the call, we will most surely crash.

After trying everything he knew, Joe called the tower and said, "Our intentions are to land, wheels down, full stop." That meant that rather than leaving our landing gear up and basically doing a belly flop landing, we would put the landing gear down and risk the left landing gear buckling under the plane. Whatever happened, the drama would soon be over. As we neared the runway on our final approach, two helicopters from local TV stations were capturing footage while a large fire truck with men wearing silver fireproof suits waited to take up chase behind us down the runway.

With everything in the cabin securely fastened and silent prayers spoken, Joe made our final approach. First he put the front and right wheels on the ground, and with great trepidation finally set the left wheel on the ground for a brief millisecond. He only had the nerve to bump the landing gear before picking it back up. He was afraid if the landing gear failed, our left wing would drop to the runway causing huge damage to his plane. Rather than folding underneath the plane, that jarring action was enough to lock the wheel into place. In that same instant, the third green light on the dash shined bright. To say we were relieved is an understatement. That green light indicated a reversal of destiny. After taxing to the hangar, workers laid out a red carpet outside our door and said, "Welcome back to earth."

While we were in our meeting with the church leadership, we had the plane checked out. Mechanics discovered that a small spring that was supposed to pull the elbow of the landing gear into a locked position had not been properly calibrated. This small thing didn't work and almost caused a crash. Often it isn't the big things that bring the greatest disasters in our lives; it's the little things. Ask God to help you find the thing that's causing you a problem, so it can be corrected. Persevere until you find it.

Sometimes making the decision to persevere and do the gutsy, right, or moral thing jars your mind and heart. It also locks in your beliefs. We only know how deeply we believe in something after we have acted on it. After suffering defeat at Ai, the excitement of starting fresh had lost its luster. The honeymoon was over. Yet, it strikes me

> JOSHUA CHOSE TO KEEP GOING, AND SO CAN YOU. HE LEARNED TO COOPERATE WITH GOD, AND SO CAN YOU.

that we sometimes have the propensity to give up or to give in too quickly. Imagine what his story might have been like had Joshua walked away from the conversation with God with a polite, "Thanks for listening, but I think I'm done." But Joshua didn't give up. He could have but he didn't. Joshua chose to keep going, and so can you. He learned to cooperate with God, and so can you.

God's promises are easily hidden when we focus on failure or setbacks. Even focusing on the prospect of failure is a dangerous thing. Acknowledge the possibility? Sure. Focus on it? No! We tend to hit what we are looking at. Doubt is always waiting to jump in front of faith. Consider that when they lost the battle at Ai they actually toyed with the idea of giving up and returning to the desert. That's ridiculous, but that's how thin faith can be. Give doubt a platform and it shouts convincingly that giving up and turning back is more desirable than moving forward.

God's vision is that you live a promised life at rest, and in victory and peace. For some of you those words may sound like make-believe. Joshua would understand because

> JOSHUA ENCOURAGES US THAT FAITH IN GOD AND NOT CIRCUMSTANCES IS THE KEY TO CONSISTENT LIVING.

his life was filled with notable opportunities to quit. Think about it. He was born into a life of oppression in which he lived for fifty years after which he lived another forty years in a wilderness because of the actions of others. Joshua didn't have the luxury to choose better circumstances, but he choose a mindset to believe God. Joshua encourages us that faith in God and not circumstances is the key to consistent living.

The last thing anybody wants to do is to fail at anything, but if you are breathing oxygen you will experience failure. This is another way that Joshua's story is our story. This third monument stands as a witness to the impact of patience and resilience.

When You Cooperate with God, He Redeems the Pile of Rocks

> *"So Joshua burned Ai and made it a permanent heap of ruins, a desolate place to this day. He impaled the body of the king of Ai on a pole and left it there until evening. At sunset, Joshua ordered them to take the body from the pole and throw it down at the entrance of the city gate. And they raised a large pile of rocks over it, which remains to this day"* (Joshua 8:28-29).

I imagine a scene in which the aged Joshua looked in the distance toward the Valley of Achor, as he spoke deliberately to a fellow Israelite, "Remember how we didn't give up? See that pile of rocks over there? Remember how we tried again and won?"

To the casual observer this monument looked like just another pile of rocks in the middle of Canaan. But to Joshua this pile of rocks represented that he hadn't given up, that he kept going. It was a reminder that he had persevered through half a century of oppression and forty years of wandering; and more recently through the fear of losing everything, the grief of losing thirty-six warriors and the doubts about entering Canaan. The thirty-six men they lost in the first battle did not die in vain. That loss was redeemed through a sweeping victory.

> GOD IS FAITHFUL AND BECAUSE HE IS, PERSEVERANCE PAYS OFF.

This third monument reminds us that God is faithful and because He is, perseverance pays off. Not sometimes. Every time. This monument should hold a sign that reads: "Failure isn't final. Try again." God is faithful to His Word. If God said He would then He will. When tough times come, just get ready because that means that your growing season has arrived. Trust God. Keep going.

Perseverance Is Rewarded

Life is filled with opportunities to quit. I'm not saying there aren't times that we should stop one thing and move to the next thing. Joshua could have given up at any point during the first fifty years of his life in Egypt because, after all, he didn't choose slavery; it chose him. How silly would it have been for him to say that he was quitting because of when and where he was born? He lived that life for fifty years. How long have you lived the life you were born into? Joshua didn't have the luxury to choose better circumstances. But he could choose to hope in the Lord, so he did. He didn't quit in Egypt and because he didn't, he got to walk out of Egypt, a free man.

Hope is a powerful thing. Hope showed up with Moses telling the people that God had heard their prayers and was going to deliver them. But it was almost one year before they left Egypt. Hope saw Joshua through that year. He didn't give up while God taught Pharaoh some lessons. His hope renewed when he spied out the Promised Land, only to have his hopes dashed as God sentenced the grown-ups to life in the wilderness. Joshua could have quit when he was sent to live in a wilderness after experiencing the Promised Land. He could have quit in the wilderness but he didn't. Because he didn't, he got to enter Canaan.

He also could have quit after this first humiliating defeat, but he didn't. Therefore he got to build another monument to God's faithfulness. Maybe you've heard the saying that most overnight successes took ten, twenty, or thirty years. Rarely, if ever, does success happen accidentally and overnight. Joshua's patience was rewarded. In the same way, your patience will be rewarded.

Beliefs >> Thoughts >> Actions >> Habits >> Character >> Destiny

Don't let your past mistakes decide your future.

Failure can be fruitful when we view it in the proper perspective: from the belief that with God, failure is not final. We can persevere through it, thinking and acting in hope towards the reward of a promised life.

Chapter 6

MONUMENT FOUR: STAY IN SPIRITUAL ALIGNMENT

"Your word is a lamp for my feet and a light on my path."

—Psalm 119:105

Smooth Driving

I DRIVE A 2006 Chevrolet Silverado. I have been known to put upwards of 36,000 miles a year on that truck. That's a lot of miles by most people's standards. I love what I do, and my job requires a lot of miles to get it done. The last time I purchased new tires I decided to get the entry-level tire because our budget was tight. The tires were rated for 50,000 miles, and I was determined to use every one of them. With average maintenance you might expect the tires to last for at least eighty- to ninety-percent of the projected miles, but there are no guarantees. In this case, I could expect between 40,000 and 45,000 miles.

At the same time the tires were installed on my truck, I also purchased a three-year alignment as well as a lifetime rotation and balance. I did it because it saved money over the life of the tires and I didn't want any excuses for not having the tires rotated and balanced at least every 4,000 miles. Each time I had the tires rotated and balanced, I also had the truck's alignment checked and corrected, if necessary. Why? Because it's important and frankly, I had already paid for it. The only part of a vehicle that comes into contact with the ground are the tires, so why not make certain that they are given a fighting chance to last?

The result impressed me. By the time I needed tires again I had put a whopping 62,500 miles on those "entry-level" tires. When I mentioned this to my guy at the tire store, he double-checked his records and found it to be true. I kept the paperwork just for those that doubt. The next time, I got tires rated for 80,000 miles. And yes, I still get regular alignments.

Spiritual Alignment

What is true of my tires is also true of us spiritually. This next monument is about alignment. Just as your tires undergo friction from their contact with the pavement, your beliefs get rubbed as they are in constant contact with culture, which means that they are in need of regular alignment. When you enter the promised life, it is essential to maintain spiritual alignment.

Spiritual alignments take a little longer than the time it takes to rotate and balance tires. God helped the Israelites defeat the people of Ai in a dramatic, strategic fashion. What did they do next? They didn't just pause for a moment. They stopped everything to worship. They got a spiritual alignment. From a practical point of view, I wonder, *Man, that must have really been inconvenient to pause for worship when you're busy conquering the land. Especially when your enemies are still pretty close in proximity.* Yet they stopped and worshiped. They listened and learned. They recommitted and offered sacrifices. This was a big deal and everyone was present—leaders, men, women, and children, and even the foreigners that lived with them.

> WHEN YOU ENTER THE PROMISED LIFE, IT IS ESSENTIAL TO MAINTAIN SPIRITUAL ALIGNMENT.

Renewing the Covenant

Renewal is something that happens just below the surface of life. Each year I renew my auto insurance, health insurance, and magazine subscriptions. I've renewed my passport as well as my estate trust. Sometimes couples have a special ceremony to renew their wedding vows. Yet no renewal is more important than our covenant with God. Israel understood this:

> *"Then Joshua built on Mount Ebal an altar to the Lord, the God of Israel, as Moses the servant of the Lord had commanded the Israelites. He built it according to what is written in the Book of the Law of Moses — an altar of uncut stones, on which no iron tool had been used. On it they offered to the Lord burnt offerings and sacrificed fellowship offerings. There, in the presence of the Israelites, Joshua wrote on stones a copy of the law of Moses. All the Israelites, with their elders, officials and judges, were standing on both sides of the ark of the covenant of the Lord, facing the Levitical priests who carried it. Both the foreigners living among them and the native-born were there. Half of the people stood in front of Mount Gerizim and half of them in front of Mount Ebal, as Moses the servant of the Lord had formerly commanded when he gave instructions to bless the people of Israel.*
>
> *Afterward, Joshua read all the words of the law—the blessings and the curses—just as it is written in the Book of the Law. There was not a word of all that Moses had commanded that Joshua did not read to the whole assembly of Israel, including the women and children, and the foreigners who lived among them"* (Joshua 8:30-35).

Build an Altar, not a Fortress

I don't know what strikes you most about that passage but for me, it sounds crazy that they read *everything* in the "Book of the Law." Are you clear about what matters most? Are you clear about the *why* behind the *what*? It is easy to get so involved with *what* we are doing that we forget *why* we are doing it. We tell ourselves that we believe the Bible is God's Word, yet I am struck by how few have ever read the Bible—all of it. The fourth monument built in the Promised Land is an altar that serves as a witness to the importance in maintaining a spiritual focus in worship and the Word. It reminds the people why they are there in the first place. You can know what you are doing and do it well; but when you know why you are doing it, you do it better.

The first battles are over, but the Israelites come a long way in a short distance. After leaving the plains of Moab and crossing the Jordan, the walls of Jericho and the people of Ai are defeated. The Israelites are beginning to take possession of the land. It would not have surprised me if the next thing Joshua did was take Shechem and fortify it, raising a fortress in the land. After all, this was the central spot in the area. Joshua, however, builds an altar, not a fortress. This altar is not the storied monument of his victories, but a reminder of God's Law. Building an altar under such circumstances is both unusual and remarkable; and yet the altar, by its inspiration, contributes more to the power of the people than any fortress could by virtue of its security. Why? Because vision and purpose inspire us more than buildings and the promise of more possessions.

> THE FOURTH MONUMENT BUILT IN THE PROMISED LAND IS AN ALTAR THAT SERVES AS A WITNESS TO THE IMPORTANCE IN MAINTAINING A SPIRITUAL FOCUS IN WORSHIP AND THE WORD.

Without delay and without caring for the unsettled state of Israel, or their enemies, Joshua confirmed the covenant of the Lord with His people. It was accomplished as Moses had directed them in Deuteronomy:

> *"When the Lord your God has brought you into the land you are entering to possess, you are to proclaim on Mount Gerizim the blessings, and on Mount Ebal the curses. As you know, these mountains are across the Jordan, westward, toward the setting*

sun, near the great trees of Moreh, in the territory of those Canaanites living in the Arabah in the vicinity of Gilgal. You are about to cross the Jordan to enter and take possession of the land the Lord your God is giving you. When you have taken it over and are living there, be sure that you obey all the decrees and laws I am setting before you today" (Deuteronomy 11:29-32).

Like Joshua, monumental leaders, desiring a promised life, don't defer committing and recommitting with God until a later time when their people feel completely safe and settled in the world. Nothing should come before worship and instruction from God's Word. The way to prosper as a leader is to begin with God.

I'm guessing you believe that's true.

I'm wondering if you live like it's true.

Our Real Fortress

"But seek first his kingdom and his righteousness, and all these things will be given to you as well" (Matt. 6:33). When Joshua built this altar he brought the religious life of the people back to life. He accomplished far more than he would have if he had built literal walls around them, or promised them iron

> NOTHING SHOULD COME BEFORE WORSHIP AND INSTRUCTION FROM GOD'S WORD. THE WAY TO PROSPER AS A LEADER IS TO BEGIN WITH GOD.

chariots and training for their soldiers. Live long enough and you'll figure out that God is a person's only real fortress. Do skill, strategy, intelligence, and knowledge matter? Yes, but they don't matter more than obedience to God. To have Him in us and around us is to be secure.

All the people of Israel, thousands of them, are standing at the base of Mt. Ebal and Mt. Gerizim. We find it difficult to focus through a thirty-five minute sermon while seated in an air-conditioned building on padded chairs. God help us all, if we ever return to wooden pews. Not only were the Israelites not sitting, which would have been considered a sign of disrespect, but in this case they were even instructed by Moses where to stand. If you go back to Deuteronomy 27-29, you will find exactly which tribes were to stand at the base of each mountain. Joshua was carrying out the directives Moses had given him. Why do this now? When circumstances start improving there is a tendency to forget the covenant we made with God: the promise to honor Him and trust Him in all things and at all times.

A Tale of Two Mountains

As with most altars, the place they were built has great significance. At the foot of Mt. Ebal was the city of Shechem where Abram had built an altar 500 years earlier.

> *"Abram traveled through the land as far as the site of the great tree of Moreh at Shechem. At that time the Canaanites were in the land. The Lord appeared to Abram and said, 'To your offspring I will give this land.' So he built an altar there to the Lord, who had appeared to him"* (Genesis 12:6-7).

The significance of this place and that moment in history would not have been lost on Joshua and the Israelites. It was here the Lord had appeared to Abram who responded by building an altar to the Lord. Later Jacob built an altar here after the Lord appeared to him in a dream (See Genesis 28:10-19; 35:1; and 48:3). Also, this where Moses encountered the burning bush. Moses built an altar too (See Exodus 3:2, 12, 16).

Joshua's altar was an acknowledgment of the sovereignty of God and how He keeps His promises, as well as a renewal of the covenant. This acknowledged they were to be devoted to God and that the land was their inheritance. It was all about the faithfulness of God. Just so you know what the big deal is: When God promised Abram that He would give him this land and lots of children, there were two huge obstacles that potentially could have stood in the way of believing it would happen. First, Abram was seventy-five years old, which is not the best time to start building a family. Second, when Abram stood at Shechem, the Canaanites populated the land, which is why it's called Canaan.

I bring that up because living the promised life isn't always having everything neatly laid out in front of us. Sometimes believing God means that I trust His promise for success, companionship and rest, even when obstacles stare me in the face. God wants His children to be obedient because He's up to something. He's fulfilling His Word and working through His plan. I don't know what obstacles are in front of you, but I know that if you'll focus on God and His Word, He will fulfill His plan in His time.

Don't let your own intelligence keep you from God. Use your intelligence to trust God. This place, these two mountains and two altars, and reading God's Word were all about being spiritually aligned.

Two Sides of Truth: Blessings and Curses

Let's get back to the altar. The altar was built at Mt. Ebal and about 500 yards away from its base was the base of Mt. Gerizim. That's the length of five football fields which is not far. As mentioned before, half of Israel stood at the base of each mountain. There are some noteworthy details given about these two mountains.

From the top of Mounts Ebal and Gerizim you could see a large portion of the Promised Land. I'm sure that was quite a sight. I don't know about you, but worship and listening to God's instruction renews my perspective of life, just like standing at the top of a mountain.

There is also a natural amphitheater that exists there. As you stand on the sides of these mountains, you can see and hear everything on both the mountains and in the valley below. Through the years many people have tested this.

They have stood on one of the mountains and had other people stand on other parts of the two mountains or in the valley. As they read something in a loud voice but without amplification, the other people were able to hear all that was spoken. It is God's own amphitheater. I can't help but think how this relates to my own act of worship. Spending intentional time in both personal and corporate worship gets me to a place in which I can hear God's Word to me.

Theologian Francis A. Schaeffer, in his book *Joshua and the Flow of Biblical Story* also points out that Ebal and Gerizim represented the very blessings and curses Joshua was reading to the people. "God had commanded that Mount Gerizim be marked the mountain of blessing and that the taller mountain, Mount Ebal, be marked as the place of warning, or the place of the curse. God was giving the people a huge object lesson: What happened to them in life was going to depend, as it were, on whether they were living on Mount Gerizim or Mount Ebal. The people were to hear from Mount Gerizim the blessings that would come to them if they kept God's law and from Mount Ebal the curses which would fall upon them if they did not."[7]

We are either living in obedience to God or disobedience. Obedience brings blessings while disobedience brings curses. I want to point out that God is not petty. He is not some cosmic being, waiting for somebody to royally mess up, so He can use one of His lightning bolts to strike them down. This is talking about willful disobedience, a lifestyle of defiance and rebellion.

Which mountain are you living on? Or do you find that you tend to divide your time between the mountains? Do you think it's impossible or difficult to live on both mountains? Consider someone who attends church services maybe weekly, while showing disregard for God in their daily family and workplace. That's living on two mountains. While that may be considered normal in your world, it's a bad plan and it's exhausting.

Atonement, Peace, and Fellowship

The people did not simply show up. They came prepared and were active participants with Joshua and with the Lord. There were two kinds of sacrifices offered at the base of Mt. Ebal: burnt offerings and the sacrificial fellowship offerings. The Hebrew word for "offering" comes from the word translated "brings." An offering is something that someone "brings" and "offers" to God as a gift. In the case of Israel, animals were brought for sacrifice or "offering."

Mt. Ebal was marked as the place of warning. Most offerings were voluntary, like the burnt offering. We know from Leviticus there were specific regulations for the burnt offerings. These burnt offerings were to be male and had to be unblemished as in all offerings. Just as He did with His Old Testament people, God desires that we offer Him our best too. Beyond merely bringing the sacrifice, the person was also to lay his hand on the head of the animal to express identification between himself and the animal (See Leviticus 16:21) whose death would then be accepted in "atonement." The whole sacrifice was to be burned, including the head, legs, fat, and inner organs, signifying the enormous cost of sin. This is why it's called a "burnt offering."

On the other hand, the fellowship offering included two basic ideas: peace and fellowship. The traditional translation is "peace" offering, a name that comes from the Hebrew word *shalom* meaning peace or wholeness. In addition to symbolizing peace between God and man, it also brought inner peace to the one making the offering. Fellowship was also involved because the person making the offering had fellowship with God and with the priest who ate part of the offering. In fact, the fellowship offering was the only sacrifice from which the one who offered it might eat a portion.

The "burnt offering" and the "peace offering" went together. To have peace with God, there had to be a blood sacrifice. Of course, for Christ-followers, Jesus Christ is our atonement. John wrote, *"My dear children, I write this to you so that you will not sin. But if anybody does sin, we have an advocate with the Father—Jesus Christ, the Righteous One. He is the atoning sacrifice for our sins, and not only for ours but also for the sins of the whole world"* (1 John 2:1-2).

Furthermore, in Christ's resurrection, we now have peace and fellowship with God. Romans 5 perfectly lays out both of these points for us today, explaining that Jesus was one sacrifice for all and in His resurrection and the Holy Spirit, we have fellowship with God.

> *"Since we have now been justified by his blood, how much more shall we be saved from God's wrath through him! For if, while we were God's enemies, we were reconciled to him through the death of his Son, how much more, having been reconciled, shall we be saved through his life! Not only is this so, but we also boast in God through our Lord Jesus Christ, through whom we have now received reconciliation"* (Romans 5:9-11).

It feels good and it is good to be in fellowship with God. When we are at peace with God, we are indeed whole. When we are at peace with God, we are spiritually aligned. Jesus Christ brings alignment because He fulfilled the requirements of the Mosaic Law,[8] and satisfied the wrath of God.[9]

> *"Therefore, since we have been justified through faith, we have peace with God through our Lord Jesus Christ, through whom we have gained access by faith into this grace in which we now stand. And we boast in the hope of the glory of God"* (Romans 5:1-2).

The Written Word

In the presence of all Israel, Joshua copied the Law of Moses on stones. Moses had ordered the people first to plaster the stones, then to write on them the words of the Law (See Deuteronomy 27:2-4). The formality of this occasion was intended to get the Israelites' attention about the seriousness and importance of the task they were undertaking. We see in Deuteronomy that the Ark of the Covenant remained in the valley between the two mountains. This was so the Lord and His Law would be visible to everyone. Deuteronomy is a covenant renewal document, filled with instructions which are designed for life in the Promised Land. The people had received the covenant while living in the plains of Moab from Moses, now was the time they were to implement it through this mass ceremony. They were doing this to make their commitment formal. Moses's instructions included the people were to respond to each blessing and curse by saying, "Amen." The Hebrew word for "Amen" means "so it is" or "let it be." By answering "Amen" the people understood and agreed with God's Word. They agreed that blessings followed obedience and curses followed disobedience. The ceremony was both formal and serious, but the intent was for a heart change in the people. It was like taking the oath of office as a president or in a court of law. A directive is spoken and a group of people answer, "I do."

One would assume that with his own hand, Joshua copied the Law of the Lord, given to Moses. Not only does this fulfill what Moses had commanded them to do in Deuteronomy 27, it also follows the instructions God had given back in Deuteronomy 17 to future kings.

"When you enter the land the Lord your God is giving you and have taken possession of it and settled in it, and you say, 'Let us set a king over us like all the nations around us,' be sure to appoint over you a king the Lord your God chooses. He must be from among your fellow Israelites. Do not place a foreigner over you, one who is not an Israelite" (Deuteronomy 17: 14-15).

*"When he takes the throne of his kingdom, he is to **write for himself on a scroll a copy of this law**, taken from that of the Levitical priests. **It is to be with him, and he is to read it all***

*the days of his life so that he may learn to revere the Lord
his God and follow carefully all the words of this law and
these decrees and not consider himself better than his fellow
Israelites and turn from the law to the right or to the left. Then
he and his descendants will reign a long time over his kingdom
in Israel"* (Deuteronomy 17:18-20, emphasis mine).

Though Joshua is not their "king," he is their leader. And knowing Joshua the way we do, he is committed to following the Lord's and Moses's instructions. I don't think this was as much out of fear as it was out of devotion. Joshua truly believed.

Re-examine Your Belief and Dedication to the Word of the Lord

Joshua believed the Word of the Lord was the way to life. He believed in the sovereignty of God and His Law. I imagine this time of copying the Law in the Promised Land reminded Joshua of his mentor, Moses, and the first time he encountered the Law. Joshua was Moses's aide, and had been allowed to travel with Moses to the base of the mountain where Moses stayed forty days and nights while the Lord's own finger inscribed the Law on two stone tablets. I imagine Joshua was one of the first people to have seen those first tablets. Joshua's firm belief in the Word of the Lord and His Law guided who he was and what he did.

> MONUMENTAL LEADERS MUST DEVELOP A HUNGER AND THIRST FOR THE WORD OF THE LORD.

What about you? Monumental leaders must develop a hunger and thirst for the Word of the Lord. This altar built by Joshua brings us back to the written Word. Remember God's first instructions to Joshua: *"Study this Book of Instruction continually. Meditate on it day and night so you will be sure to obey everything written in it. Only then will you prosper and succeed in all you do"* (Josh. 1:8, NLT). If obeying the Word of God brings blessings, then disobeying the Word of God brings curses. We cannot just accept what sounds good to us and throw out the rest.

Written by forty authors, over multiple generations on three continents and in three languages over 1,400-1,500 years, the sixty-six books of God's Word should be inscribed on a leader's heart. Why? It is our Prototype #27.

Prototype #27

In Washington D.C., there is a building called the National Institute of Standards and Technology. This facility is responsible for storing perfect samples of weights and measurements. They have what are called "prototypes" of pound weights and kilograms as well as measuring rods for feet, yards and metric measurements.

There, one can find a "meter standard," which is a reinforced bar of platinum alloyed with exactly ten-percent iridium. When they want to know the exact measurement of a "meter" they cool this bar down to 0 degrees Celsius (the melting point of ice) at a sea level of 45 degrees latitude, then they know they will have the exact tip-to-tip measurement of a meter. That bar is known as "Prototype #27": The US received National Prototype Meters No. 27 and No. 21 in 1890. The original is kept in a suburb of Paris at the International Bureau of Weights and Measures.

The written Word of God is our Prototype #27. The Bible acts as the spiritual measuring rod that never changes. Paul wrote to the young preacher Timothy about the usefulness of Scripture:

> *"All Scripture is God-breathed and is useful for teaching, rebuking, correcting and training in righteousness, so that the servant of God may be thoroughly equipped for every good work"* (2 Timothy 3:16-17).

Do you believe to your core that the Bible is inspired? I'm not going to spend time convincing you. There are several books that already do a great job of this. I recommend John Clayton's "Does God Exist?" webpage at www.doesgodexist.org. The best books I know are *How to Read the Bible for All Its Worth* by Gordon D. Fee and Douglas Stuart or *Evidence for Christianity* by Josh McDowell. If you are a faithful follower of Christ and a leader in your home, church and community, you already believe in the Word, but I'd like to remind you of its proof of inspiration—to build your resolve to know it and follow it.

The Word Teaches

The Bible offers correct information. To be taught is to learn something you did not already know. The Bible is able to give knowledge and information inspired by God. Like any good manual, the Bible gives principles for how to live life. Yet it is more than a good manual because it is inspired. The Word of God is our religious authority.[10] The Word of God is also complete.[11]

John Clayton was raised by atheists, but came to faith in Christ. He writes this about his experience with the power of God's Word:

"I had been told by several people as a child that if you ever become a Christian, you cannot ever be happy; you cannot ever own anything; and you have to walk around with a long sad face and your chin dragging on the ground. Yet when I read the Bible, I read statements like, *"So ought men to love their wives as their own bodies. He that loveth his wife loveth himself. For no man ever yet hated his own flesh; but nourisheth and cherisheth it..."* (Eph. 5:28-29, KJV, *reference added*). I read about the Ethiopian eunuch who went on his way *rejoicing* because he had found Jesus Christ and the happiness that went with that acceptance of Jesus in his life. I have had many problems come into my life, but all I have to do is to look back at how miserable life was without Christ and I can realize that life, as it is now with Jesus, is beautiful in comparison...It is amazing to me that as I talk to people, I find many who claim to be Christians and who perhaps claim to have been Christians for many years who have not read the Bible through cover to cover once. I find it hard to believe that they believe in God very much if they do not even want to know what He has to say." [12]

The Word Rebukes

Did you know that sailors do not fear storms, but they do fear cloudy nights because they can't see the stars? They lose their ability to chart their course. Scripture has a way of un-clouding our vision of ourselves. As humans, we tend to think too highly of ourselves. God's Word has the power to stop my wrong ways of thinking, clear my vision, and send me in a new direction, as if I were headed south down the interstate when I should have been going north.

> GOD'S WORD HAS THE POWER TO STOP MY WRONG WAYS OF THINKING, CLEAR MY VISION, AND SEND ME IN A NEW DIRECTION

We see this kind of rebuke in the book of Mark. Jesus is telling the disciples about His impending death and resurrection. Peter rebukes Jesus for saying these things and then Jesus rebukes Peter.

> *"He spoke plainly about this, and Peter took him aside and began to rebuke him. But when Jesus turned and looked at his disciples, he rebuked Peter. 'Get behind me, Satan!' he said. 'You do not have in mind the concerns of God, but merely human concerns'"* (Mark 8:32-33).

When Jesus rebuked Peter, it was to stop his wrong way of thinking. He still cared for, and loved, Peter. Peter was wrong and needed to be put straight. When the Word of the Lord rebukes us, we need to stop what we are doing and turn around—do a complete 180.

According to the Center for Bible Engagement, ninety-seven percent of Americans do not know God is speaking to them through the Bible. What a sad reality. This means a lot of Christians have things backwards. How about you? Does your theology (what you know about God) inform your life (the choices you make daily) or does your life inform your theology? Augustine, the famous fifth century theologian, is quoted as saying, "Where Scripture speaks, God speaks."

The Word Corrects

This might sound like a rebuke, but it's not. Think of it as a course correction. You are going in the right direction, but you need to be steered a little more to the left or the right. As we drive a car, we make constant corrections without thinking, not because we are dangerous drivers but because we are safe drivers. First-time drivers also make corrections as they drive, but they are stiff, rough, and sometimes feel dangerous. As we mature and drive more, we learn how to better negotiate a light that is changing from green to yellow at an intersection. We learn how to keep a safe distance on the highway, and what tailgating is and is not. The longer we stay in God's Word, the better we will self-correct. Hebrews 4:12 reminds us:

> "For the word of God is alive and active. Sharper than any double-edged sword, it penetrates even to dividing soul and spirit, joints and marrow; it judges the thoughts and attitudes of the heart."

My character and your character are flawed. Sometimes we are headed northeast and we need to veer more towards true north. We see Jesus doing this when the lawyer approached Him, asking what the greatest commandment was. The man knew it was to love God and to love your neighbor as yourself. Jesus told him his answer was right, but then went on to clarify the point about loving your neighbor as yourself with the parable of the Good Samaritan. He corrected the man's course of thinking through the parable. Jesus concluded His teaching by asking:

"'Which of these three do you think was a neighbor to the man who fell into the hands of robbers?'

The expert in the law replied, 'The one who had mercy on him.'

Jesus told him, 'Go and do likewise'" (Luke 10:36-37).

The Word Trains in Righteousness

Did you know there is a World Happiness Report? It is published by the United Nations Sustainable Development

> THE QUALITY OF THE PROMISED LIFE IS CONNECTED DIRECTLY TO OBEDIENCE TO GOD.

Solutions Network and it measures the "happiness" or quality of life in different countries. Data is collected from people in over 150 countries. According to the 2016 report, Denmark is the winner.[13] What is the quality of life index for the Christian? Living the promised life! The quality of the promised life is connected directly to obedience to God. If we obey, blessings will "overtake" us. If we do not, catastrophe will "overtake" us.

This is not to say that the life of even the most obedient and righteous believer will be without difficulty. In His great teaching on obedience in Matthew 7:24-27, Jesus made it clear the house built by the wise man, the one who both hears and obeys His teachings, would stand firm and strong even while being rocked by the winds and rains of life's storms. And isn't that the true measure of our quality of life: contentment?

Proverbs 19:23 says, *"The fear of the Lord leads to life: then one rests content, untouched by trouble."* In Philippians 4:12-13, Paul writes, *"I know what it is to be in need, and I know what it is to have plenty. I have learned the secret of being content in any and every situation, whether well fed or hungry, whether living in plenty or in want. I can do all this through him who gives me strength."*

Joshua Reads ALL the Law

When Joshua internalized the Law by copying it down, he was prepared to read the Law to all the people—the aged, the children, the warriors and the women. God wants intelligent service for all. Ignorance is the mother of superstition, not of devotion. *"God is a Spirit, and they that worship him must worship him not only in Spirit"* that is, in sincerity; *"but in truth"* (John 4:24, KJV): that is, with intelligence, understanding Him, and giving Him the honor and respect He deserves.

There is no need to keep truth from people. Truth is good for us, whether we know it or not. Some leaders talk of a God of love, but forget that a God of love is also a holy God who punishes sin. Whether I believe in gravity or not, it's still present and true. Ignoring it does not make it go away or change it. And if I do not accept it as a fact, I am not going to fly anytime soon because gravity is real. God's nature is just as absolute. He is a God of love and a God of holiness. In my opinion, if God does not punish sin then He's a God of hate instead of love. When we hide the truth of punishment or danger, we are not acting in a loving way. We should fear partial truth. In this ceremony Israel embraced all truth. We should embrace complete truth too. Embracing total truth is part of living the promised life.

> THERE IS NO NEED TO KEEP TRUTH FROM PEOPLE. TRUTH IS GOOD FOR US.

God is in Your Midst

As the words of the Law were read, God was in their midst. Have you ever listened to God's Word being read and felt like God was speaking directly to you? I know I have on many occasions. This reading of the whole Law of God was one of those times. It was not a formal ritual of some kind. This had been planned out and thought through with Moses himself. It was a celebration of what God had done and was doing. We know God's presence was recognized because the Ark was there. Truthfully, the entire celebration would have been a sham had it not been carried on in God's sight. Finally, to be acceptable to God, the devotion of the hearts present was required.

In churches around the world today, it's easy to become enamored with worship to the point that you can find yourself worshipping worship, rather than the God for whom it is intended. Maybe a question worth considering is this: Is church supposed to be pleasing to Him or to you? There is nothing innately wrong with lights shining through haze or videos playing behind talented worship leaders and bands. And there is nothing wrong with singing from a hymnal with an organ or singing a cappella while reading words on a screen either. The point is that when God's Word is read aloud or sung or read privately, it should be done wholeheartedly. It should not be done as a weekly performance to get

> MAYBE A QUESTION WORTH CONSIDERING IS THIS: IS CHURCH SUPPOSED TO BE PLEASING TO HIM OR TO YOU?

our attention. Our hearts must be engaged with Him, desiring at the deepest level of our being to trust and obey Him as our Lord and Savior first. God will not push His way into our lives. Why would He? Instead He stands at the door and knocks, and if we will open the door, He will come in. God is always an invited Guest or He is not present at all.

Worship that is acceptable to God requires a devotion of the heart. There should be a passionate desire on man's part to benefit from His Word. Reading God's Word doesn't impress God because God already knows what He said. He doesn't really need to be reminded of what He said. He isn't forgetful. We are though. We need to be reminded of God's promises. We need to agree with them and act accordingly.

It does no good to simply agree. To believe God without putting what we learn into action is as worthless as a three-dollar bill. When God's Word is read publicly or privately, it should not be an intellectual exercise. Whenever we approach God's Word with anticipation that God is going to speak to us, our ears are opened to His voice. Our eyes search for truth and know it when we see it.

Jesus warns us about reading the Scripture without recognizing the presence of God in our midst:

> *"You study the Scriptures diligently because you think that in them you have eternal life. These are the very Scriptures that testify about me, yet you refuse to come to me to have life"* (John 5:39-40).

The purpose of the Word of God is to give life. How is His Word giving you life?

Captain's Log: Journaling with God's Word

James Tiberius Kirk, the famous Starfleet commander of the *USS Enterprise* on Star Trek always kept a captain's log. The log was used to inform the captain's superiors of what was happening on a mission and to record historical facts for future generations. I think Psalms reads a bit like a captain's log. King David wrote about the ups and downs of life. The Psalms are raw, poetic, and offer guidance. They often help me stay the course or get into spiritual alignment during difficult times.

One of the most difficult decisions I've faced came to a head as 2011 dawned. I was wrestling with whether or not to leave a ministry I had invested in for more than twenty-one years. With the encouragement and support of my wife, I met with a trusted, professional counselor on January 25, 2011. It wasn't the first time we had met and it wouldn't be the last. While I didn't know it at the time, my final Sunday at that ministry would be Christmas later that year.

During this particular visit on January 25, I had a lot of questions to fire at the counselor: "How come they can't do... Why won't they consider...?" ("They" were the people I was struggling with.) My counselor calmly explained that these were not helpful questions. To be honest, in addition to my litany of questions, I had a dump truck load of anger. In response to my questions, confusion, and anger on that Tuesday afternoon, my counselor gave me an assignment.

He said, "I want you to study Psalm 13 and apply it to your current situation. Meditate on it. Write about it." He wasn't done. Knowing my propensity to study the Bible for the purpose of teaching others, and knowing my desperate need to grow and benefit personally from the hardship I was facing, he added: "I want you to agree that you will not teach or preach what you are learning." He asked me to journal what happened. What were my thoughts and behaviors? What emotions did I feel? Was I hurt, frustrated, or bitter? He also wanted me to pray, thanking God for those around me.

Looking back at my journal I am reminded of the wisdom that my counselor shared and the reason for the assignment. My counselor said: "A change of environment won't fix things, but as you change, a change of environment may be necessary to do the next great thing in your life. God is going to drive you and break you to make you what He wants you to be. Remember, you are to be a sacrifice for God's good pleasure. The incense from that sacrifice goes to His nostrils. A broken and contrite heart is what He wants. Then and only then will God move them (referring to my current leaders) or He will move you."

Then, taking on the voice of God, my counselor said, "You just think that was the rodeo. Oh no, it wasn't. Wait until I break you, then watch how useful you will be to Me."

I wondered privately to myself: "Does God have an easier time breaking certain people? Is it possible that I am too hurt to leave, or am I simply not strong enough to leave? Did my brain's hardwiring tell me that leaving was simply not an option?"

I took the advice of my counselor and began reading and writing. In my journal I wrote a simple prayer to start: "God, give me wisdom. Make me sensitive to Your touch." I read the assigned passage and let what King David was saying, sink in.

Here are my journal entries:

David's writing in Psalm 13:

> *"How long, Lord? Will you forget me forever?*
> *How long will you hide your face from me?*
> *How long must I wrestle with my thoughts*
> *And day after day have sorrow in my heart?*
> *How long will my enemy triumph over me?"* (Psa. 13:1-2).

Oh, God, how often have I asked "how long?" How I have longed for relief. Waited for relief. Wanting to let go, move forward, be patient, stay, help improve the situation all at once. How long? Forever? Will it ever change?

I look to my thoughts only to find that mixed with any hope I might have is a constant sorrow. I look to receive counsel from myself but it seems unclear and uncertain and hopeless. From where I sit and according to my understanding, my enemies are winning and I am losing. Is this how it ends? David wonders and I wonder too.

I am angry and demand answers.

More from Psalm 13:

> *"Look on me and answer, Lord my God.*
> *Give light to my eyes, or I will sleep in death,*
> *And my enemy will say, 'I have overcome him,'*
> *And my foes will rejoice when I fall"* (Psa. 13:3-4).

Is it possible for me to have a new perspective? I wonder how many people never receive a new perspective and cease to truly live? I don't want to live this kind of life. I want to choose another life. I wonder...how many people exist day-to-day in darkness, confusion, frustration, full of sadness and hopelessness? How many? And is it because God does not see them or perhaps that He does not care? Is it that I do not see what God wants me to see? Am I incapable of seeing the things of God?

It just seems that the harder I try, the further behind I fall while my enemies seem to thrive. Meaningless! The double-edged sword for sure.

Psalm 13 and the Key to Life

> *"But I trust in your unfailing love;*
> *my heart rejoices in your salvation.*
> *I will sing the Lord's praise,*
> *for he has been good to me"* (Psa. 13:5-6).

I believe that this is the key to life! Trust in God's love. If you need a refresher, you might review Chapter 2. Whatever I may be going through, it is because God loves me or either God does not exist. I

> WHATEVER I MAY BE GOING THROUGH, IT IS BECAUSE GOD LOVES ME OR EITHER GOD DOES NOT EXIST.

don't see any gray area here. And I do not like it. I believe that I am supposed to love God with all of my heart, soul, mind, and strength. But what does that mean? It can't possibly mean that I feel good about God. It definitely means more than that. I think it means that in any moment, I must be able to say that I trust Him. I trust that the circumstances are there because He loves me. I trust that His discipline has purpose. I trust that when I am hurting because of my choices and not only His, that God's love brings with it forgiveness, grace, faithfulness and mercy.

How do I know if I am trusting God? I think that to trust is to be content in that moment. And it is also to be able to say "thank you" to the Lord for everything. This is the essence of true spirituality. And when I am able to say thank you I am able to rejoice because I know that it all turns out for my salvation.

> IT DOESN'T TAKE MUCH OF GOD'S WORD TO CHANGE YOU, BUT IT DOES TAKES GOD'S WORD.

Perhaps I am saved from my current enemies, perhaps not. But I will rejoice in His salvation even before I experience it.

And because I am now at ease in Him, I sing. Think about how natural it is to sing when we are happy and at ease. To trust in something is one thing. To trust in the One who holds all power and is with us is another.

As I look back at my journal, I am reminded that it doesn't take much of God's Word to change you, but it does takes God's Word. There is power in the process, and alignment is sometimes aggressive, but it's necessary.

Developing Rhythm

Just as metronomes are used for musical practice, keeping the musician in rhythm, so God's Word keeps you faithful to the truth. The Israelites had a calendar of feasts and celebrations, including altars and sacrifices. There was a rhythm God put in place for them. How do we make this practical for us because we don't have an altar? It has been a long time since we've brought a sheep to the priest. How do we sacrifice today? How do we willingly bring things to God? We must sacrifice our rights and our time, developing a rhythm in life that puts God's Word at the centrality of our being.

> WE MUST SACRIFICE OUR RIGHTS AND OUR TIME, DEVELOPING A RHYTHM IN LIFE THAT PUTS GOD'S WORD AT THE CENTRALITY OF OUR BEING.

There is probably no other story that has illustrated this for me better than that of Mitchell Ray Palmer Sr., and his daughter, Cindy. I met Cindy after preaching in Leesburg, Florida, on loving the Word of God.

Mitchell began preaching when he was thirty, Cindy told me. He was described as highly educated, highly motivated, and a sound gospel preacher. He and wife, Betty, had three children: Cindy, Ray, and Michelle. Like most parents, they faced the ups and downs of raising kids. And like most parents, they worked hard at having their children turn to God's Word for answers to life's problems, challenges, and questions. They were being faithful to train their children to love

God and His Word, all the while unaware of the tragedy about to strike and just how important those lessons would become.

It was the Saturday after Thanksgiving, 1974, and the Palmer family was on a 250-mile drive home to Alabama from visiting friends in Tennessee. Less than 100 miles into the drive home, an eighteen-wheeler crossed into their lane and hit them head-on. Mitchell Ray Sr., was killed instantly. Betty Palmer died an hour later. Cindy, age 15, Ray, age 14, and Michelle, age 10, were all taken to a hospital in Jackson, Tennessee. A month following the accident, Michelle died from the injuries she sustained.

As Cindy recalled her life story to me and was expressing her deep love for the Word of God, I wondered aloud, "How can fifteen- and fourteen-year-olds lose their parents and a sister, yet still love God and His Word so much?" She shared that her parents had always encouraged them to seek answers in the Scriptures. They would have them read the Bible, study a subject, and then return to discuss what they had found. "When I read and found, I believed," Cindy said.

She went on to tell me how she is passing this same love of God and His Word to her children, Bridgett and B.J. (then ages 14 and 7). Bridgett came home from a Wednesday Bible class, asking, "Does God know what choices I will make in the future?" There were two teachers in the class. Bridgett told her mother one teacher had answered "yes" and the other had said "no." And the class was left that way—with two different answers. Cindy referred Bridgett to a psalm in which David spoke of God knowing. Bridgett went off to read and study and returned. Bridgett decided God does know but does not miraculously influence your decisions. She said to her mom, "It's like a parent knowing what their child will choose."

Cindy had followed the same simple, effective formula with her daughter that her parents had built into her. This mom has confidence that if she should ever be away from her children the way her parents were, her kids will know where to turn for answers to life's questions and challenges. This is both maintaining spiritual alignment *and* establishing a spiritual legacy.

It would have been understandable if Joshua had built a fortress instead of an altar that day between the two mountains. But that one misstep could have gotten the Israelites out of alignment. We, too, must find a way to maintain a spiritual focus, so we don't lose our way, or veer off the path. Developing a rhythm in life that allows for times of intentional silence and solitude to study God's Word is the only way to stay focused on living the promised life. Silence, solitude and study are our allies, not our enemies.

Cindy's story reminds me that we as leaders can't afford to lose our way. Others are counting on us, especially our children. In life, everything often looks identical in priority. How can we know what matters most? How do you decide if one thing is more important than another in any given moment? Spiritual alignment means that we are in a position of agreement with God. To be in agreement with God, we must know Him and His Word. The better the alignment, the less wear and tear we feel.

Centered

If all the monuments were laid out on the floor, this fourth monument would be in the center. I picture picking up this monument of spiritual alignment, and all the other monuments are hanging off it, to the left and the right, hence it represents that God's Word should be at the center of my life. It is the connection that holds all the other monuments together.

When I am spiritually aligned, all the other monuments are easier to grasp. Likewise, when this monument is missing there seems to be a void, leaving the monuments disconnected. The reason for this is that each monument requires faith to trust God's Word. God's Word is useful for helping me to know my next step as well as helping me to see further along the road of life that I'm on. This may be what the psalmist had in mind when he wrote: *"Your word is a lamp for my feet, a light on my path"* (Psa. 119:105). Whenever I encounter doubts or difficulties it guides me. Whenever I combat fear and feel stressed or discouraged about the future, the Word of God lifts me up. God's Word is a guide showing me the way and an anchor for the soul.

Beliefs >> Thoughts >> Actions >> Habits >> Character >> Destiny

Has your belief in the power of God's Word turned into
a dedication to it?

What actions or habits are evidence of that?

How is God's Word forming your character and determining
your destiny?

Chapter 7

MONUMENT FIVE: ACCEPT RESPONSIBILITY...EVEN WHEN IT HURTS.

"Therefore each of you must put off falsehood and speak truthfully to your neighbor, for we are all members of one body."

—Ephesians 4:25

Life Is Peppered with Mistakes

I COME FROM a large family. With five kids, three girls and two boys, things were always happening. We never had much in the way of worldly possessions, but we always had enough. Since money "doesn't grow on trees" as Mom would say, I really don't have memories of our entire family eating a meal at a restaurant, except for this one particular time at the Pancake House.

Before Interstate 40 was built, one of the first restaurants you'd come to on the famous Route 66 through Winslow, Arizona, was the Pancake House. I don't remember the occasion that led to this meal out, but it must have been special. The restaurant was packed and I remember we were seated at a round booth. I sat beside my brother, David, who is five years younger than me.

While Mom and Dad prepared to place our order, I noticed the pepper shaker and came up with a way to occupy my time. I put some of the pepper in the palm of my left hand, and asked David, "Do you want to sneeze?" He said sure and asked me how. I explained that having pepper blown into his face would cause him to sneeze. Before you start judging me, let me say that I had seen it in the Saturday morning cartoons, so I knew that it must be true. I had no idea what was about to happen.

"Are you ready?" I asked my little brother. He nodded his little head yes. Holding my hand flat out in front of his face, David smiled and held his eyes wide open. As I blew the pepper into his face, David let out the loudest, shrillest cry I had ever heard.

As you can imagine, our family became the center of attention at the Pancake House. I was sure my brother was living his final "seeing" moments on earth. I wanted to disappear, and I wished I could take it back. With intention and great accuracy, I had blown pepper into David's eyes, completely unaware of its possible consequences. What I now understand is the small particles in pepper called capsaicin not only burn and irritate, they can be sharp and scratch the cornea.

My dad knew what to do. He jumped up, grabbed David, and as he headed for the bathroom, he commanded me to come along. This didn't feel right at all. In the bathroom, Dad simultaneously washed out David's eyes with copious amounts of water and asked me what I had done.

"I blew pepper into his face. I didn't know it would burn!" I answered my dad with a squeaky, fearful voice.

"Why?" he asked.

"He was supposed to sneeze! I don't know why I did it!" I admitted.

Dad believed me and I promised I would never again blow pepper into anyone's face. I had blown it big time with that pepper. (Pun intended.)

Have you ever made a mistake like that? Maybe you were naïve, gullible, or ignorant of the risks or consequences. Learning to live with mistakes is a skill that everybody needs. It's not *if* you'll make a mistake; it's *when*. Part of maturing as a person is learning from mistakes. I can promise you that I've never blown pepper at anyone ever again and have no plans to do it.

There are so many valuable lessons surrounding this fifth monument because it's all about making mistakes and how God redeems them. I have broken this chapter into two parts. Part one focuses on that fact of life we all hate to admit: that everybody makes mistakes, even monumental leaders! Part two will focus on what God can do with those mistakes: miraculously redeem them! So, don't stop halfway through, discouraged by your mistakes. As in life, you have to keep digging in with the Lord until the end to see the miracle.

Part One: Everybody Makes Mistakes

There are three different kinds of failure and we can learn from each. First, there are slips or missteps—those things we do completely unintentionally. However, even those have consequences. Have you ever mistyped a word when you're texting, even though you knew how to spell it? Or typed the text correctly about how you don't care for your boss, only to discover that you sent it to your boss? To err is human, as the saying goes. However, being human doesn't erase the consequences. Although unintentional, some slips can have catastrophic consequences, such as accidentally pulling the trigger of a loaded gun.

Second, there are violations—when someone intentionally breaks the rules. What Achan did was in clear violation of God's Law. As we went over in Chapter 4, a sign that you are violating something can be that you hide the truth from others. It's exactly what Bernard "Bernie" Madoff did when he created up to an estimated $50 billion of losses for investors, which is said to be the biggest fraud committed in the history of Wall Street. For that he was sentenced to 150 years in prison.

Third, there are mistakes—things you do on purpose but with unintentional consequences. The good news is God will not abandon us because of them. Sometimes it is as simple as a bad decision. We must live with the consequences.

Make the Call

Whether you are a leader at work, in your home or at church, there is something you do every day: You make decisions, not only for yourself, but for your people. You might be asked a dozen questions a day, requiring you to make a call.

"Can I go out with my friends after school?"

"Will you sign here, finalizing the purchase?"

"Should we help this person with their rent payment?"

"Who should we hire?"

"Who should we fire?"

People look to leaders to take the first step and have the final word on a matter. Decisiveness is a key ability in leadership. Because leaders are faced with more decisions than non-leaders, we get the opportunity to make more mistakes. As wise old Uncle Ben says to young Peter Parker (a.k.a. Spider-Man), "With great power comes great responsibility."

Our decisions have consequences, don't they? Some are positive and some negative. With one "yes" or "no" the fate of the people we lead can end in success or failure. Such was the case for our leader and mentor Joshua in this next part of his story. Just as my heart ached for Joshua when someone on his team sinned (Achan), my leader's heart hurts for what is about to happen next. We can all identify with being deceived or making a mistake that has a negative consequence, albeit unintentional.

Deception Happens

I received a phone call offering me a "free trip" and I fell for it. I gave my credit card number and was charged $100 for this "free trip" but received nothing at all. There are people who make their living from deception. The Gibeonites used it to literally save their skins. All the kings west of Jordan had heard about the Israelites' success, especially about the walls of Jericho coming down. That was a real shocker and got the attention of those on the entire coast of the Mediterranean Sea, as well as those in the hill country and the western foothills. Fearing for their own lives, the kings in the area came together, making a plan and a pact: all except one group—the Gibeonites. They formulated their own plan. Joshua 9:4a says, *"they resorted to a ruse...."*

A Gibeonite delegation approached the Israelite camp, pretending to come from far off, asking for a peace treaty. The truth is they were very close neighbors, trying to get protection and possibly provision from their powerful new neighbors.

And Joshua believed them.

> *"Then Joshua made a treaty of peace with them to let them live, and the leaders of the assembly ratified it by oath"* (Joshua 9:15).

The Hebrew noun for "peace" used here not only means the absence of armed conflict, but *friendship*, thereby guaranteeing their safety.

The Enemy Does His Homework

The Gibeonites were persuasive because they had done their homework and knew a lot about the Israelites. They knew how to build up Joshua and his fellow leaders. They planned every detail of their lie, even bringing moldy bread, hoping to show they had made a long journey. The Gibeonites said exactly what the Israelites wanted to hear:

> *"...Your servants have come from a very distant country because of the fame of the Lord you God. For we have heard reports of him: all that he did in Egypt, and all that he did to the two kings..."* (Joshua 9:9-10a).

The Gibeonite delegation told the Israelite leaders their reputation was great and everybody had heard about God's success—even from far away. If you read all of Joshua 9, you will note the enemy said nothing about Israel's victories at Jericho and Ai, not wanting to give away that they were neighbors.

Not only did Joshua fall for the ruse, all the leaders did. All the leaders of Israel sampled the provisions of the Gibeonites and came to the same conclusion. Not one of them thought for a moment this might be a trick. Sometimes a lot of smart, well-informed, and successful people can agree, and still be wrong: like when President Bush was told that Iraq had weapons of mass destruction, or leaders are duped by manipulated global warming data.

We can be tricked as well. If only Joshua could have fact-checked the Gibeonites story at Snopes.com. We even have a new term these days called "fake news." Fake news seems legitimate because it's talked about as though it is, but it's not real. It's fake.

There was another reason Joshua and his leadership team were duped. It was a subtle, yet bigger, mistake.

The Bigger Mistake: Not Inquiring of the Lord

The enemy has the power to deceive. That is certain and can be traced back to the garden of Eden. You will never be too important or intelligent that you will become incapable of being deceived. I'd go so far as to say that if you believe you can never be deceived, you already are—self-deceived. Paul warns, *"But I am afraid that just as Eve was deceived by the serpent's cunning, your minds may somehow be led astray from your sincere and pure devotion to Christ"* (2 Cor. 11:3).

So how can we see deceit when it comes our way? Joshua learned the hard way that the only way to deal with this kind of attack was to seek God in every situation. Scripture says:

> *"The Israelites sampled their provision **but did not inquire of the Lord.** Then Joshua made a treaty of peace..."* (Joshua 9:14-15a, emphasis added).

God is on His throne, waiting to be consulted, and we ignore Him at great risk. This failure was contrary to the explicit instructions the Lord gave to Joshua concerning how to discern His will, that they should consult Him.

Refer back to Monument No. 4 about maintaining spiritual alignment. During the transfer of leadership from Moses to Joshua, there were explicit instructions given about how to inquire of the Lord in making decisions.

> *"He [Joshua] is to stand before Eleazar the priest, who will obtain decisions for him by inquiring of the Urim before the Lord. At his command he and the entire community of the Israelites will go out, and at his command they will come in"* (Numbers 27:21).

That process obviously didn't happen in this situation with the Gibeonites. Joshua and the Israelite leaders confirmed the Gibeonite claim purely in their own strength and on their own initiative. It seems to be human nature to drop our guard when things are going well. Perhaps we've reached a certain position or influence, and think too much of ourselves. Or maybe we get too busy to wait on the Lord or to take the time to "inquire of the Lord." These leaders were guilty of what Charles Pfeiffer calls "excessive credulity and culpable negligence."[14]

For everything a leader can know in making a decision there are still important details you or I may not know. Within three days of making this treaty, the Israelites learned the truth about the Gibeonites. Unlike the last time things went wrong, this time Joshua knew exactly what he had done. He had made peace with the enemy.

Like the Gibeonites, Satan's goal is to deceive and confuse us. We get busy or preoccupied and forget that we are in a spiritual war and have an Enemy out there. Deception is his primary tactic and scheme, and we can fall for it. It is why Paul warns us, *"Put on the full armor of God, so that you can take your stand against the devil's schemes"* (Eph. 6:11). Are you inquiring of the Lord in every circumstance or decision to be made?

Leaders, we need to realize that we *"have not because"* (we) *"ask not,"* as James 4:2, KJV, says. That verse came to life for me when I became friends with

Mrs. Mattie Brooks, a precious lady in her seventies whose faithful example in prayer has taught me a lot. "Dan, you have not because you ask not!" she would say to me in a matter-of-fact tone. And when she prayed, Mattie's requests were filled with thanksgiving, as though God had already answered! That is the prayer that moves mountains, folks! Remember what Hebrews 11:6 promises: *"he rewards those who earnestly seek him."*

Within the many layers of this fifth monument are important lessons. When you've tasted success, don't lose sight of the mission and the responsibility to inquire of the Lord. When mistakes happen, don't let those who would deceive you define who you are. And as we will see, God was not angry with Joshua for making this mistake. Nor did God remove the consequence of his mistake. Sometimes the result is that we must live with our mistake. And with God on their side, the Israelites were able to make the mistake work for them, instead of against them.

Don't Pass the Buck. Act with Integrity.

Joshua didn't pass the buck by blaming someone else when the deception was uncovered. Blame never helps. He took full ownership of the mistake. When you own the problem, then you can fix the problem. Joshua stood with integrity even under criticism. He and the leaders honored the covenant with the Gibeonites. The fact that the men of Israel were deceived did not remove the responsibility from them.

Yes, they kept the peace treaty intact with those stinking, lying, neighboring Gibeonites! It would have been easy to shirk responsibility out of self-protection, but Joshua would not undermine his leadership in that way. When the nation set out to war like they had planned, they came to Gibeon but did not attack them *"because the leaders of the assembly had sworn an oath to them by the Lord, the God if Israel"* (Josh. 9:18).

Joshua could have reasoned the alliance was based on false information, and therefore not binding upon them. I think we would all give a pass to

Joshua, should he have decided the treaty invalid. The Gibeonite deception was a pretty huge loophole the Israelite leaders could have slipped through. But Joshua kept his word. That, my friends, is leadership under pressure. Our commitments should mean something as well. I wonder if the great King David had this story of Joshua in mind when he penned this psalm. He writes,

> *"Lord, who may dwell in your sacred tent? Who may live on your holy mountain?...the one...who keeps an oath even when it hurts..."* (Psalm 15:1,4).

Make Your Mistakes Work for You

Even as he kept his oath, Joshua did not let the Gibeonites continue as an independent nation. Joshua tells the Gibeonites:

> *"'You are now under a curse: You will never be released from service as woodcutters and water carriers for the house of my God'"* (Joshua 9:23).

There were consequences for their deceit. Joshua allowed the Gibeonites to reap what they had sown. He literally gave them what they asked for. This may seem cruel to us, but there is a kindness in the cruelty. Remember the Gibeonites, in their deception, chose servitude rather than death. Whenever they asked Joshua to make a treaty with them, they were offering to submit themselves and be subjects to the Israelites. Their decision to accept the terms of being woodcutters and water carriers brought them into contact with the knowledge of the true God. Joshua and the leaders did not wallow in self-pity over their mistake, nor did they let anger overtake them and strike out against the Gibeonites. They made the mistake work for them—literally.

And you know what? The Gibeonites agreed to serve. The one part of their original story that held some measure of truth was their fear of the Israelites. They responded to Joshua:

> *"So we feared for our lives because of you, and that is why we did this. We are now in your hands. Do to us whatever seems good and right to you"* (Joshua 9:24b-25).

Mistakes have impact and consequences that outlive us. Consequences can be positive or negative. Such is the case of the Gibeonites mixing in with the Israelites. Your associations matter. There's no evidence in Scripture the descendants of the Gibeonites created long-term problems for the Jews.

Another way to make your mistakes work for you is to acknowledge them and allow the memories of those mistakes their proper place. Don't forget them, but don't let them hold you back either. Have you done things you regret? Sure, we all have. You may even feel shame for something in your past. While mistakes and poor decisions are part of our story, they don't need to be the end of it. Keep living. Start another

> GET YOUR GIBEONITES UNDER CONTROL, AND MAKE THEM SERVE YOU WHILE YOU SERVE THE LORD.

chapter and keep writing your story. The proper understanding of our mistakes humbles us. I imagine that in some ways having the Gibeonites hanging around all the time was bittersweet. They did work, but their presence was a reminder of Joshua's mistake. You know the saying, "Those who forget the past are doomed to repeat it."

Joshua wasn't afraid of the truth that he had been deceived. When he realized it, he acted accordingly. He did not hide from it and pretend it had not happened. To find truth and not change is to be self-deceived.[15] We are not to ignore our mistakes, but we should not let them cripple us or keep us from being useful in the future either. Everyone makes mistakes, so get your Gibeonites under control, and make them serve you while you serve the Lord.

Part Two: Re-examine Your Beliefs about the Power of God's Grace

Do you believe God forgives and He is a merciful God? Do you believe He does this more than once? That He not only saves you for eternity, but from your everyday mistakes, big and small? Oftentimes people in leadership need to be reminded that God's grace is for us too.

I remember sitting in the back row of a conference in the mid-2000's at Willow Creek Church in Chicago. The building was packed. Pastor Bill Hybels was closing the conference and invited a lady to end the event with an a cappella version of "Amazing Grace." I remember Bill telling the leaders that we spend so much time helping others heal, that it is easy for us to forget that God's amazing grace is for us too. I thought to myself, *Well, this is a good way to close a conference*, but I wasn't overly captivated by the whole idea—until she started to sing. Tears started streaming. I was falling apart at the magnitude of God's grace and calling. God never asked me to be perfect. He asked me to lead.

> I THINK IT IS WORTH NOTING THAT GOD IS NOT EXTREME; HE DOES NOT MARK OUR MISTAKES AND TELL US TO KEEP THEM BEFORE US.

Although this alliance with the Gibeonites was a poor decision, the Lord was still with Joshua and the Israelites. I think it is worth noting that God is not extreme; He does not mark our mistakes and tell us to keep them before us. God didn't place a big black X on Joshua for his error, and He doesn't place it on us either. King David, who had experienced God's mercy, wrote: *"If you, O LORD, kept a record of sins, O Lord, who could stand? But with you there is forgiveness; therefore you are feared"* (Psalms 130:3). God is for you! God distinguishes between human infirmity and human depravity. A mistake may complicate your life, but not devastate it.

1 John 1:7 is a foundational verse in my life, shaping my beliefs, thoughts, actions, habits and character.

"But if we walk in the light, as he is in the light, we have fellow-
ship with one another, and the blood of Jesus, his Son, purifies
us from all sin."

We walk in the light, meaning that we walk towards truth! So admit your
mistake, but keep walking. Jesus is the One who purifies us from all sin. He
does not just forgive, but purifies. He does not mark us as unworthy when we
make a mistake. He keeps on walking right next to us instead, lifting us up,
urging us on, as we walk into truth.

When your young child makes a huge mess with a bowl of spaghetti, you
don't just forgive them for the mess, you clean it up. God forgives and helps
with the clean-up too. It doesn't always mean there won't be the natural consequences, but He is with us. John was adamant we understand this concept
so He said it again just two verses later this way:

"If we confess our sins, he is faithful and just and will forgive us
our sins and purify us from all unrighteousness" (1 John 1:9).

No Failure Is Beyond God's Ability to Redeem

What I admire about Joshua in this next part of the story is something
everyone looks for in a leader: integrity. Joshua walked with integrity. He
wasn't afraid of people knowing he had made a mistake. However, his mistake
was compounded whenever the Gibeonites became a target because of their
peace treaty with the Israelites. The Amorite king of Jerusalem, Adoni-zedek,
appealed to all the kings in the surrounding area to form an alliance against
the Gibeonites and the Israelites, with the city of Gibeon being the first target.
Who did the Gibeonites call for help? Joshua, of course.

Here is where things got serious. Would the Israelites honor the oath they
had made or would they turn their backs on the Gibeonites? Would the
Israelites be true to their word, or had they just been giving lip service to them?

Joshua remained true to his covenant with them and relieved the city, pursuing the attackers. Sometimes the wrong decision leads you to defending what you otherwise would have defeated. Defending the city of Gibeon was less about the Gibeonites and more about the Israelites defending their vow.

Although Joshua was facing unintended consequences of his decision, that didn't stop him from doing the right thing. Joshua responded with strength, courage and obedience. God, as promised, was with Joshua. Joshua took the entire army including his best fighting men.

> SOMETIMES THE WRONG DECISION LEADS YOU TO DEFENDING WHAT YOU OTHERWISE WOULD HAVE DEFEATED.

They didn't just "sort of" defend the Gibeonites. They went all in. Don't allow unintended consequences to stop you from giving your very best.

Joshua made a mistake but that didn't stop God from fulfilling his promises. The Lord was with them in this fight, saying to Joshua, *"...I have given them into your hand..."* (Josh. 10:8). They marched all night to take the enemies of Israel and Gibeon by surprise. *"The Lord threw them into confusion before Israel, who defeated them in a great victory at Gibeon"* (Joshua 10:10a). Joshua not only *gave* his best, he also *did* his best, to resolve the threat as soon as possible. They defended the city of Gibeon and had great victory, but it didn't stop there.

Israel continued to pursue the enemy and the Lord sent hailstones to seal the deal. According to Joshua 10, *"...and more of them died from the hail than were killed by the swords of the Israelites"* (Josh. 10:11). Joshua didn't ask God to do this. In fact, it likely would have never occurred to Joshua to ask for hail to fall on the enemy. The timely occurrence of the hail was a miracle, but an even greater miracle was the fact that the stones *hit only the enemy soldiers.* God knew that his people were doing their best and that they needed His help. It's important to take notice of how the Lord is working to make you successful with what He's asked you to do. In what ways have you noticed God working on your behalf?

God took His special "ammunition" out of His storehouse and used it to good advantage. When God's people obey God's will, everything in the universe works for them, even the *"stars in their courses"* (See Judges 5:20, ESV). When we disobey God's will, everything works against us. (See Jonah 1 for a vivid illustration of this truth.)

Ask For the Impossible

Hailstones weren't the only miracle in this story. While the hailstorm was helpful, there were other real factors at work. Joshua's men were exhausted after marching all night and fighting all day. Joshua needed a special act from God because he knew that if night came, the enemy could escape. It may have been that Joshua had learned his lesson about ignoring the Lord, because this time he prayed to the Lord in front of all Israel:

> *"Sun, stand still over Gibeon, and you, moon, over the Valley of Aijalon"* (Joshua 10:12).

And that is what happened. This was no figure of speech. The sun and the moon stopped until the Lord and the Israelites had decimated all their enemies. *"There has never been a day like it before or since, a day when the Lord listened to a human being. Surely the Lord was fighting for Israel!"* (Josh. 10:14). Can you imagine the front page of the next morning's paper? What a headline! "Lord listens to Joshua! Earth stops rotating!"

How do you explain a miracle, any miracle? Of course, the simplest answer is the answer of faith. Jeremiah 32:17 (NLT) says, *"I am the Lord, the God of all mankind. Is anything too hard for me?"* Day and night belong to God (See Psalm 74:16), and everything He has made is His servant. Think of it in this way: If God can't perform the miracle described in Joshua 10, then He can't perform any miracle, including the miracle that stands at the heart and foundation of Christianity, the resurrection of Jesus Christ from the dead. Do you want to serve a God who can only act in ways that you can understand and explain? To say that God can create, but cannot perform miracles, is to say that

He imprisoned Himself in His own creation. I have a difficult time believing in that kind of a God.

C.S. Lewis wrote, "The mind which asks for a non-miraculous Christianity is a mind in process of relapsing from Christianity into mere 'religion.'"[16]

Like Joshua, each of us must find balance to contend with real life difficulties and challenges as we fulfill God's will for our life. On the one hand, God is sovereign, and on the other, I have personal responsibility. For me that balance is found in this:

I trust God can and will provide everything I need to accomplish what He's asked me to do;

and

He gives me strength to do what I should do.

This brings me to one of my favorite verses couched in a great Old Testament story about a leader named Nehemiah. He was commissioned to rebuild the walls of Jerusalem. In the middle of construction, Nehemiah received threats from those who opposed it and were planning to attack them. His response was this: *"But we prayed to our God and posted a guard day and night to meet this threat"* (Neh. 4:9). When Nehemiah heard trouble was imminent, he prayed to God and posted a guard. The old adage attributed to Saint Augustine would apply here, "Pray as though everything depended on God. Work as though everything depended on you." Nehemiah, like Joshua, did two things, and so can we. First, he asked God for help. Second, he posted a guard. Faith and action working together. Faith and action create balance that brings success over challenges.

Stay On Mission

Whenever you feel overwhelmed, remind yourself that God is never overwhelmed. That means that when doubt and fear threaten to inundate your thoughts, God is right there waiting for you to ask for His help. He won't allow anything to overcome, overpower, or overrun you so that you are destroyed. As the five kings conspired against Joshua, *God in heaven must have laughed (Psa. 2:1–4),* because unknown to them, God was using their plan to accomplish His own purposes. Realize too, that not even Joshua realized all that God was up to. His job was to be strong, courageous and obedient and to trust that God was working out His part. God used Joshua's mistake with the Gibeonites to protect Gibeon and accelerate the conquest of Canaan. Instead of having to fight five smaller "nations" at five different times, Joshua would now fight all five at once.

As the battle progressed, the five enemy kings, realizing they were losing, hid together in a cave. When Joshua was told about this hiding place, he had large rocks rolled over the mouth of the cave and guards stationed there. He also told the army to continue pursuing the enemies all the way back to their cities.

> *"So Joshua and the Israelites defeated them completely, but a few survivors managed to reach their fortified cities. The whole army then returned safely to Joshua in the camp at Makkedah, and no one uttered a word against the Israelites"* (Joshua 10:20-21).

Joshua remained focused on his mission and, because he did, he was victorious. While there were many armies to overcome, he concentrated on the one directly before him. Once the Israelite army returned to the camp at Makkedah, probably the next day, Joshua ordered the cave be opened and the five kings brought to him. *"When they had brought these kings to Joshua, he summoned all the men of Israel and said to the army commanders who had come with him, 'Come here and put your feet on the necks of these kings.' So they came forward and placed their feet on their necks"* (Joshua 10:24).

Joshua then called for his officers to put their feet on the necks of the kings to symbolize not only victory but also of the victories the Lord would give His people in the days ahead. The kings were slain and the five corpses hung on five trees until sundown. Then their bodies were put into the cave, with a pile of stones closing up the entrance. Joshua's next words must have inspired the hearts of his courageous soldiers.

> *"...Do not be afraid; do not be discouraged. Be strong and courageous. This is what the Lord will do to all the enemies you are going to fight"* (Joshua 10:25).

Do those words sound familiar? They echo the *70 Seconds* when God spoke to Joshua as he prepared to enter the Promised Land. Joshua was reminding them to stay on their mission, and we must do the same because we are promised success just as Joshua was. Whatever battle or mistake you are facing, don't be afraid. Continue to go back to the basics of strength, courage and obedience. God promises us companionship, rest and, success, even when we royally mess up. Move past the shame and embarrassment of your mistake. Make your mistakes work for you.

Create a Pattern of Consulting God, But Don't View God as a "Consultant"

While this story is a great example of a bad decision which leads to a good outcome, this doesn't justify the mistake or make mistake-making desirable. Joshua acted thoughtlessly and not systematically in his first interaction with the Gibeonites. Joshua acted without consulting God. That's understandable. After all, who hasn't made at least one dumb decision, even if it was based on faulty information? Joshua was out of step with his normal pattern of behavior and relationship with the Lord. Joshua's habit was to consult God because he depended on God and he had wholly surrendered to God. God was more than a "consultant" in Joshua's life. Is God more than a consultant that you keep on retainer to help you out from time to time in your life?

Joshua had seen Moses consult with the Lord time after time. Joshua did not act systematically as though there was no God at all. To act systematically without God is to bring failure after failure into your life. Living this way places

God under you, not on the throne. After a while, without a change, systematically acting foolish will bury you under a mountain of failure that no amount of success or change in attitude could easily overcome. It can only be turned around when the systematic behavior of poor decision-making has stopped. There are some practical things that can be put into place in our lives, so that over time we will develop new habits. Here are a few to put into place:

Decide to Attend Services with the Church Every Week. This is an opportunity for you to participate in communion, which focuses your mind on Christ, as well as an opportunity to hear God's Word from another perspective other than your own. And hang around a bit because it will also afford you the opportunity to get to know other Christians and have fellowship.

Begin Each Day Talking to God. Give thanks to Him and ask Him for wisdom and insight for the challenges ahead. Ask Him to make a way, to intervene, and work in ways that only He can because He's God. Invite God to do His part and then do your part as well.

Begin the Day Reading at Least Five Minutes of God's Word. Deliberately stop participating in mindless, worthless and empty conversations whether in person or over social media platforms. Begin with the Word of God first. Let it be the first thing you put in your brain every morning. It will help you face the day and transform your thinking.

Keep a Journal so You Are Able to See Answered Prayers and Stay Focused. Trust God to do His part and you do yours. Answered prayer is incredibly encouraging and faith-building. The record you keep will bless you.

Victory Doesn't Always Follow a Straight Line

That pile of stones in front of the cave holding the dead kings' bodies is the fifth monument. Another strange monument? Yes, it was. There was great victory, but victory didn't follow a straight line. This story can't be told to future generations without exposing the colossal poor decision-making made by the

Israelite leaders. God paved the way towards victory despite the mess men had made. It is a monument to our humanity and God's faithfulness.

Beliefs >> Thoughts >> Actions >> Habits >> Character >> Destiny

Do you believe in God's power to alter the outcome,
even when you've messed up?

Do you move forward in faith or shrink back in fear?

Do you honor your word to others as Joshua did?

Are you spending time with God in prayer and His Word every day?

If this has fallen by the wayside, begin again! Remember, God
is FOR you!

As God works for the good in your life, keep a record so that you too
can point to the victories He brings out of our mistakes.

Trust Him. He loves you.

Chapter 8

MONUMENT SIX: PURSUE PEACE

"If it is possible, as far as it depends on you, live at peace with everyone."

—Romans 12:18

"Get Over It!" and Other Advice Husbands Should Not Give!

YOU LEARN A lot about pursuing peace from being married, especially if you've been married more than one day. At the time I wrote this book, Beth and I have celebrated thirty years together now. We not only love each other, we also *like* each other. Even in the best of relationships though, peace is not always present. We must pursue it. It was June 17, 1994, Beth and I were hosting a party for young single adults from the church. As it turned out, I had double-booked myself for that evening. Not only were we hosting a young adult party, I would be leaving before the party ended for a leadership retreat. Not good planning on my part.

My job for the party was to grill the chicken. Before everyone was scheduled to arrive, I noticed the racks in our grill needed to be cleaned. There's no time like the present, right? In the eleventh hour, I started cleaning the racks from the grill in the kitchen sink, which had already been cleaned for the party. Needless to say, Beth didn't agree that cleaning the grill racks...in the kitchen sink...at that time...was the best idea.

Words came tumbling out of my mouth. "Get over it!" I blurted. She was speechless. I had never spoken to her that way ever before. In that moment, I was already pretty sure I would never say those words again.

For clarification and in an attempt to be helpful, I added, "The party will run itself."

Then she spoke, "Since the party will run itself, I'll leave."

With that, she walked to the bedroom, got her purse and car keys, and headed for the garage. Now, you need to know something about my wife. She does not bluff. She has healthy boundaries. I realized how much I needed her and my plan was, indeed, not working. I hadn't intended to offend her, but that was an irrelevant detail at this point. I was headed toward becoming part of the singles group I was about to host.

As Beth walked toward her car, I begged her to stay. I went Old Testament on her, pleading for forgiveness, ready to put on sackcloth and pour ashes over my head if needed. Beth decided to stay and I decided to stop talking—the best decision I made all day.

In Pursuit of Peace

This isn't the only time I have offended my wife in our thirty years of marital bliss, but it is certainly one of the most memorable moments for both of us. Offending people, either intentionally or unintentionally, is a fact of life. Sin has flawed the human race, making us self-centered, thus, we will not always be at peace with one another. It's why the Bible tells us over and over to seek peace...to pursue it. The Bible goes so far to as to say this: *"Whoever of you loves life and desires to see many good days, keep your tongue from evil and your lips from speaking lies. Turn from evil and do good; seek peace and pursue it"* (Psa. 34:12-14). And it is repeated in 1 Peter 3:10-11.

> LIVING IN HARMONY WITH OTHERS MAY BE THE MOST OVERLOOKED, BUT MOST NEEDED, LESSON ON WHAT IT MEANS TO LIVE AND LEAD BY FAITH IN GOD.

The sixth monument is about living in peace with others. Living in harmony with others may be the most overlooked, but most needed, lesson on what it means to live and lead by faith in God.

Relationships Are like Icebergs

If you ever go on an Alaskan cruise, you will get to see some massive icebergs. Did you know that what you see of an iceberg above the water is usually only one-ninth of its actual volume? Remember the Titanic? Everything was fine. The ship was making good time until it hit an iceberg that ripped a hole in the hull of the ship. It wasn't what they could see that was the problem; it was what they couldn't see.

It's the same way with relationships. One day everything can be smooth sailing. The next thing you know, something happens that threatens to sink the unity. No wonder we use the expression "tip of the iceberg" when describing a problem or difficulty that is only a small manifestation of something much larger. Most of what a relationship is about is below the surface. Relational icebergs can be dangerous to navigate. From my experience, people either learn how to communicate effectively or they stay stuck.

From Battle Plans to Peaceful Lands

This sixth monument was built seven years after the journey across the Jordan River into the Promised Land. You will recall from the last chapter, that the fifth monument was the victory over the five Amorite kings. After that fifth monument, the battles were not over. There were kings and kingdoms to be defeated first to the south and then to the north. Finally, after the northern enemies of Israel are defeated, in Joshua 11:23b it is written, *"...then the land had rest from war."* This is followed by a list of defeated kings in Joshua 12.

It was time for the Israelites to move their mindset from battle plans to living in peaceful lands. But as we will see, that transition wasn't a piece of cake or a walk in the park. Joshua began the process of assigning the land among the tribes as Moses had instructed.

Dividing the Inheritance

Joshua 13-21 records a detailed account of the boundary lines set forth by Moses for every single tribe to receive an inheritance of the Promised Land, except Levi. The tribe of Levi was given no inheritance, as they were to live in cities and be taken care of by the offerings made to the Lord. We'll talk more about that later in this chapter. There seems to be no dispute about who gets which part of the Promised Land. This is a good leadership lesson in and of itself. Make a plan and communicate the plan ahead of time. The first three tribes to receive land were Reuben, Gad and half of Manasseh. These men finally got to go home.

Going home? Didn't they just move into the Promised Land? To go forward in this story, we must look back. Numbers 32 records a situation between Moses and the leaders of the tribes of Reuben, Gad and half of Manasseh. These tribes were shepherds and the land they were currently living on, not the Promised Land, was a good fit for their flocks and herds. These tribal leaders approached Moses, asking if they could stay there and not move their families into the Promised Land across the river.

Moses was angry at this request. I would print out his furious words, but Moses lectured these tribes for a good fifteen verses, even calling them a "brood of sinners!" I imagine that once Moses finally took a breath from his rant, the tribal leaders saw their chance to explain:

> "...We would like to build pens here for our livestock and cities for our women and children. But we will arm ourselves for battle and go ahead of the Israelites until we have brought them to their place. Meanwhile our women and children will live in fortified cities, for protection from the inhabitants of the land. We will not return to our homes until each of the Israelites has received their inheritance. We will not receive any inheritance with them on the other side of the Jordan, because

our inheritance has come to us on the east side of the Jordan"
(Numbers 32:16-19).

As they explained their request and their continued commitment to all of Israel, Moses started to see things in a little different light. Clearly he was still angry, but now he had a better understanding of their motives and plan. He still took a minute to threaten and curse the tribes, should they renege on their agreement to defend their brothers across the river. It is interesting to note that the fighting men of Reuben, Gad and that half of Manasseh were the first to cross the Jordan, marching into battle.

Appreciate a Promise Fulfilled

The men of Reuben, Gad and half of Manasseh who had settled on the other side of the Jordan did as they promised. They fought alongside their brothers and sisters, defending the nation, even though their homes were not in the same jeopardy. Joshua summoned these two-and-a-half tribes, also known as the eastern or transjordan tribes, before they depart for home and delivered one of the best farewell speeches ever. Joshua said,

> *"...You have done all that Moses the servant of the Lord com-*
> *manded, and you have obeyed me in everything I commanded.*
> *For a long time now—to this very day—you have not deserted*
> *your fellow Israelites but have carried out the mission the Lord*
> *your God gave you. Now that the Lord your God has given*
> *them rest as he promised, return to your homes in the land*
> *that Moses the servant of the Lord gave you on the other side*
> *of the Jordan. But be very careful to keep the commandment*
> *and the law that Moses the servant of the Lord gave you: to*
> *love the Lord you God, to walk in obedience to him, to keep his*

commands, to hold fast to him and to serve him with all your heart and with all your soul" (Joshua 22:2-5).

Herein lies another leadership and relationship lesson within the pages of history. We should enjoy times of peace and use those times to invest in relationships. To live in harmony with others, it is important to communicate appreciation, publicly and privately. Commending others should be the first thing on our relationship checklist.

There are lots of methods to show appreciation to others. None of them are wrong and all are better than nothing. I've commended others through a timely letter, a short note in a card, a pat on the back, a text, a phone message, and even through e-mail. I've also passed along compliments through others, knowing that my words would eventually hit the intended target.

Why did Joshua commend these tribes in this way? Joshua publicly appreciated these men for the work they had done. The work to which God had called them was difficult, demanding and dangerous; and although they didn't realize it at the beginning, it would take them seven years to complete. It demanded perseverance. I imagine that there may have been times when they felt like packing their bags and going home; times when they got homesick and wanted to go back to their families. But

> FAITHFUL SERVICE SHOULD NEVER BE TAKEN FOR GRANTED. IT SHOULD BE RECOGNIZED AND APPRECIATED.

they didn't. They kept their word to the Lord and their brethren, so, before they left the Promised Land, Joshua said thank you.

Faithful service should never be taken for granted. It should be recognized and appreciated. Each time you communicate appreciation to someone, you are making deposits into the relationship bank between you.

Twenty Years in Ministry

It was my twentieth anniversary, in 2009, of being the senior minister at the Metro Church. The leaders of the church had planned a very nice sit-down meal in my honor. They flew my mother in from Phoenix, a last-minute surprise for me. The place was packed and I was humbled. I must admit that it was nice to hear good things said about me, and before I was dead. Though I was in a season of ministry that was hard, these words of encouragement and honor have stayed with me. I even enjoyed the ribbing and roasting that went on that night as well.

One particular man's words are precious to me even to this day. Tom Jarzynka stood and reminisced about the funeral I had done for his son, Zac. It was the largest funeral I had ever done. Zac, and his girlfriend, Brittany Smith, both in high school, had died in a tragic car accident together. "They were two of the most popular and polite kids at Oviedo High," wrote Mike Bianchi in the *Orlando Sentinel*, on May 17, 2002.[17] People stood in line five hours to pay their respects and grieve with both families.

Zac and his brother had come often to our church with their mother, but Tom rarely, if ever, attended with the family. In the weeks following the funeral, Tom and I talked a lot about God, Jesus, and baptism; and spent lots of time in specific Bible study. It was a blessing to baptize Tom.

Now, seven years later, Tom stood to speak at the church dinner in my honor. He said, "When people care for others the way this church cared for me and my family, it comes from the top down. It's not an accident." Looking at me, he continued with a simple, "Thank you."

It's wonderful to see people who are thankful for you and what you do. Sometimes appreciation is the juice that keeps you going one more day. Gratitude can also act like glue, holding together a hurting marriage, a strained friendship, or a difficult work relationship. Philippians 4:6 says, *"Do not be anxious about anything, but in every situation, by prayer and petition, **with thanksgiving**, present your requests to God"* (emphasis mine).

I can't help but wonder if Joshua's appreciation to these eastern tribes set the tone for their well-meaning actions during the journey home we read about next.

Homeward Bound with Good Intentions

The eastern tribes leave Shiloh, headed for home. On their way to Gilead, they stop at Geliloth along the banks of the Jordan and built a huge altar. The altar was a replica of the altar of the Lord that stood at the tabernacle at Shiloh. It appears to have been much larger than the real thing. The altar mentioned was so large that it was referred to as *"imposing"* (Josh. 22:10).

It was likely a raised platform upon which offerings were made. We will learn later that their motives for constructing the altar were pure. However, it appeared to everyone else that the eastern tribes were already turning away from God's instructions. It was a Titanic moment, when the relationship between the eastern tribes and the western tribes was about to sink! Joshua 22:11 describes the clash:

> *"And when the Israelites heard that they had built the altar on the border of Canaan at Geliloth near the Jordan on the Israelite side, the whole assembly of Israel gathered at Shiloh to go to war against them."*

I cannot overstate just how explosive this situation was. The enormous altar overshadowed the good intentions of the eastern tribes. The western tribes logically assumed the altar had been built to offer sacrifices, and God had told the people to destroy the altars they found in the land of Canaan. No one was to build a separate altar for offering sacrifices.

Gossip always sounds true, doesn't it? It didn't take long for word to spread about this altar and strong assumptions to form. The western tribes immediately assumed this was for the purpose of establishing another center of worship where sacrifices would be offered to God to save the eastern tribes from travelling to Shiloh.

A+ for Caring

The western tribes do get an A+ for enthusiasm and a sincere desire to honor God. Their zeal is commendable, even if misplaced. They overreacted to the altar, but at least they cared enough to react at all. This is a pretty good change from the past, when the Israelites fell prey to worshipping foreign gods and made golden calves. Even so, the building of an altar was a big deal because it was something God had forbidden. He had said there was to be only one altar in Israel and that altar would be established at the place that He appointed.

> *"But you are to seek the place the Lord your God will choose from among all your tribes to put his Name there for his dwelling. To that place you must go; there bring your burnt offerings and sacrifices...Be careful not to sacrifice your burnt offerings anywhere you please. Offer them only at the place the Lord will choose in one of your tribes, and there observe everything I command you"* (Deuteronomy 12:5-6a, 13-14).

We often have a relaxed view about worship, and a lack of knowledge of Scripture on the subject. We may be inclined to think: *What's the big deal? If someone wants to build an enormous altar, let's call it art and move on.* But God didn't look at it that way. The western tribes cared appropriately, but almost acted hastily.

The moment word reached them that somebody in Israel had committed apostasy the western tribes armed themselves. They didn't hold a meeting or worry themselves as to the reason why their brothers would do such a thing. They got up and set out to do something about it. While it's good they were not afraid to speak up and they were concerned about obedience to God's commands, the call for war was based on an assumption, on what appeared to be solid evidence. After all, there was an actual altar built that was not supposed to be there, wasn't there? Based on the evidence at hand, war seemed a logical response. The word used here for war is a reference to the complete destruction of everything, not only human life. They weren't going to mess around. This was a no-holds-barred, all-out, nothing-survives kind of war.

Talk *to* People, Not about People. Assumption Is the Absolute Lowest Form of Knowledge

Call it what you want—assumption, rash judgment, misunderstanding, jumping to conclusions—all are common occurrences in relationships in families, churches, or businesses today. This is a classic example of the saying: "Shoot first, ask questions later."

A mob mentality is a dangerous thing because a mob has no mind of its own. These battle-tested warriors were ready to kill their brothers because of a misunderstanding. This is often the result when we let our emotions take over our reason.

In our pursuit of peace, it's important to get all the facts, remembering there are always two sides to every dispute. Have you heard of the Ladder of Inference?[18] It is natural to draw conclusions about others when we observe their actions or experience behavior without ever having had a conversation with them about that behavior. This happens in a flash as we select data from the pool of all available data, and infer and assign a motive that seems to fit. We've all done this.

> IN OUR PURSUIT OF PEACE, IT'S IMPORTANT TO GET ALL THE FACTS, REMEMBERING THERE ARE ALWAYS TWO SIDES TO EVERY DISPUTE.

Based on our inferences, we make assumptions, which lead to conclusions, thereby solidifying our beliefs about a person or group of people. See how we are climbing a ladder here? We live everyday as though certain things are true, even if they are not. We assume that certain things *will* happen, not that they *might* happen. With certainty, our assumptions become our truth, even if they may be false.

You know the saying: "When we 'assume' we make an 'ass' out of 'u' and 'me.'" Assumption is the absolute lowest form of knowledge. Yet we do it all the time and often unconsciously.

Past Mistakes Are Hard to Forget

Thankfully in the Israelites' case, cooler heads prevailed and the two sides talked before they fought. Everyone necessary was present at the meeting. Phinehas, the son of the high priest Eleazar, was part of the delegation from the west that went to speak to the tribes of the east. With him were ten representatives: one head from each family division among the Israelite clans in the west.

Phinehas almost blew the conference before it got started because instead of listening, he began pointing out their failures and making serious accusations. Phinehas said,

> *"The whole assembly of the Lord says: 'How could you **break faith with the God of Israel** like this? How could you turn away from the Lord and build yourselves an altar in rebellion against him now? Was not the sin of Peor enough for us? Up to this very day we have not cleansed ourselves from that sin, even though a plague fell on the community of the Lord! And are you now turning away from the Lord? If you rebel against the Lord today, tomorrow he will be angry with the whole community of Israel. If the land you possess is defiled, come over to the Lord's land, where the Lord's tabernacle stands, and share the land with us. But **do not rebel against the Lord** or against us by building an altar for yourselves, other than the altar of the*

Lord our God. When Achan son of Zerah was unfaithful in regard to the devoted things, did not wrath come on the whole community of Israel? He was not the only one who died for his sin"' (Joshua 22:16-20, emphasis mine).

Today we might be surprised by the intensity of Phinehas's emotions. The situation with the eastern tribes triggered memories in him, so Phinehas brings his case against the eastern tribes right away, reminding them of how much was at stake and just how deadly God's wrath could be. People had previously died in situations very similar to the one at hand.

The first example he mentioned was the enormous sin of Peor—a place where the Israelites fell prey to the Moabite worship of the false god, Baal. The prophet Balaam was instrumental in leading the people of Israel into apostasy, away from God. As a result, 24,000 Israelites were killed by an epidemic; they were all still suffering because of that (See Numbers 22-25). Interestingly, Phinehas was an eyewitness to this event in Peor, so this was hitting close to home for him. The second example Phinehas offered was the sin of Achan and everyone knew how that turned out.

> WE NEVER KNOW WHAT CAN TRIGGER AN EMOTIONAL RESPONSE IN PEOPLE, LEADING THEM TO ANGER, FEAR, OR SOME OTHER STRONG RESPONSE.

We never know what can trigger an emotional response in people, leading them to anger, fear, or some other strong response. Growing up, my mother didn't just warn her five kids about using alcohol. She was strongly opposed to alcohol of any kind. Now that I am older I realize why. She grew up with an alcoholic father. When she was a child, she would sometimes run to a neighbor's house in fear, because her father could be a mean and abusive drunk. She has good reason to warn us about drinking.

When you understand the source of someone's emotion, you have a new appreciation for the intensity of the situation and their opinion. The only way to understand intensity like this is to listen, ask questions, and not respond in haste yourself.

Speak Up with Humility

Phinehas must have paused his rant for a moment, because the eastern tribes finally got the chance to speak. I'm impressed the eastern tribes graciously showed restraint and held their tongues while these accusations were made. They didn't lose their tempers and fly into a rage. When their opportunity to speak came, they explained the reason why they had built this altar—not as an alternative to the altar at Shiloh, but as a

> EFFECTIVE AND LOVING COMMUNICATION SOMETIMES HONESTLY CONFRONTS, ALWAYS LISTENS, AND WILLINGLY EXPLAINS INTENTIONS AND MOTIVE WITH HUMILITY.

memorial and witness to their essential unity with their brothers on the other side of the river and their commitment to the worship of the true and living God.

This provides another lesson in leadership communications: Don't be afraid to speak up. Sometimes we need to speak up because our actions have been misunderstood. Effective and loving communication sometimes honestly confronts, always listens, and willingly explains intentions and motive with humility. If someone has made an incorrect assumption about you, gladly explain yourself.

Sometimes we will do things in life that cause a lot of stress and anxiety in others which we never intended. We leave ourselves open to the misunderstandings of others. This is when we expect them to be psychic and somehow know we had good intentions.

It would have been easy to tell Phinehas to take a long walk off of a short pier. But the eastern tribes had as much to do with this misunderstanding as the ten western tribes did. The building of the altar was not a good idea.

To their credit, they responded humbly. In essence, they said, "God Almighty knows what our motives were. He alone is to be praised. If we have done what you said, then we deserve God's punishment and more, but we did not do what you have said. We did not build this altar to sacrifice on it, or to worship another god. We built this altar simply as a witness." (See Joshua 22:22-23.)

They also admitted they built the altar with a little fear in mind, saying to paraphrase, "We were afraid that in many years to come, your children might tell our children, 'you have no part in worshipping God, because the Lord has made the Jordan River a boundary between us.' We want our children to be able to say, 'See that altar on the other side of the river? Our fathers put it there as a witness to indicate that we all worship the same God and come from one people even though the river divides us.'" They built that altar to remind future generations to be true to God. The last thing on their minds was turning away from God (See Joshua 22:24-29).

What a tragedy it would have been if the eastern tribes had responded arrogantly. When we love one another, we really do have to explain our motives and be willing to accept the righteous motives of others. If you find yourself saying, "I don't have to explain myself!" then there's a good chance you're choosing to destroy that relationship. What do you have to lose by explaining your motives anyway?

Transitions Are Hard

We fear change. The eastern tribes were afraid they'd be forgotten and the western tribes feared repeating past mistakes and God's wrath. In this case, the east and the west came to an understanding regarding the matter of the altar. However, in life just because someone is nice about explaining the motive for a given action, does not mean that we are required to agree with him or her. While building the altar was not sin, it was also not necessary. Why? Because all Israelite males were required to appear at the sanctuary three times a year

(See Exodus 23:17). This alone would preserve the unity of all the tribes, both spiritually and politically. Good intentions to improve something can actually complicate it.

This new life the Israelites were about to experience was exciting, but times of transition are hard. Transitional moments sit on the full spectrum of emotions, from exciting to scary, like...

...when your parents are aging.

...when new leadership comes.

...when kids leave home.

...when a baby is born.

...when you move.

...when you're graduating.

Moments like these are almost always fertile ground for misunderstanding and miscommunication. Are you in such a transition? How are you pursuing peace?

Re-examine Your Beliefs about Others

Psalm 34:14b says to *"...seek peace and pursue it."* Peace is a worthy pursuit. Our holy God sought to make peace with us and wants us to have peace with one another. But if peace is going to happen, it will require effort. That effort begins in you and your basic belief about others. Philippians 2:4 says, *"Each of you should look not only to your own interests but also to the interests of others. Your attitude would be the same as that of Christ Jesus."*

> THE BEST WAY TO PURSUE PEACE ON A DAILY BASIS, NOT JUST IN TIMES OF TROUBLE OR TRANSITION, IS BY CONSTANTLY POSITIONING (OR REPOSITIONING) OUR HEARTS SO THAT WE PUT OTHERS AHEAD OF OURSELVES.

The best way to pursue peace on a daily basis, not just in times of trouble or transition, is by constantly positioning (or repositioning) our hearts so that we put others ahead of ourselves. What would happen if you assumed the best about others? What if your opinions and facts were put on the back burner for a time, so you could gain understanding of a person or situation before you acted or spoke in a situation?

I find it interesting the motive behind the actions of both the western and the eastern tribes was God's holiness. But in their haste, their unity was almost destroyed. Thankfully, both sides were humble enough to explain themselves and change their actions.

Remember the grilling conflict I had with my wife that started this chapter? The root of our fight, or rather, my stupidity, was my selfishness. I wanted to do things my way and in my time. I neglected to consider my wife as better than myself. I neglected to consider her words as wiser than mine, her plan better than mine. I have a long list of "what I wish I had done" actions. I wish I would have...

...listened to Beth.

...stopped what I was doing in the kitchen sink.

...put the grill back together.

...asked how I could help with the party set-up.

Thank goodness she offered me grace, giving me a do-over. If you start thinking of others as better than yourself, the pursuit of peace will get easier and your actions will follow your beliefs. What are signs that you are becoming a leader who pursues peace? Hopefully, you will find yourself doing the following more often.

Eight Peace-Pursuing Actions

1. You believe the best about others.

To live in harmony with others, it is important to avoid jumping to conclusions. If you are pursuing peace, you will avoid passing judgment based on mere outward appearances. You'll be slower to judge someone's motives based only upon what you see or hear. The western tribes jumped to conclusions, even though their eastern brothers had fought side by side with them faithfully for seven years.

Even if something stinky might be going on, treat people with dignity and respect, allowing them the liberty to hold divergent views or give them the space to explain themselves.

2. You are willing to risk the relationship.

Often our society encourages individualism to the point that it is easy to develop an apathetic attitude toward our brothers and sisters in Christ. It's a "live-and-let-live" worldly attitude. Phinehas cared so much about his relationship with God that he was willing to risk the relationships with his brothers over it, when he could have been apathetic. In pursuit of peace, you will love God and the other person enough to pursue peace, even if it means risking the relationship. This is one thing the eastern tribes got right. They cared enough about everyone's holiness to make it an issue.

If you are a peace-pursuing leader, you will not have indifference toward others. You will act in love and courage, going humbly and frankly to a friend and asking for an explanation, even if what they did seems indefensible.

3. You know how to apologize.

Rarely is the strain in a relationships as one-sided as we want to believe. If you are pursuing peace, you will ask yourself, "How have I contributed to this conflict?" There is great power in an apology. Sometimes saying "This was my mistake. I'm sorry" can take a load off our backs, or turn around a situation altogether, allowing us to start over. The bottom line is this: When tension rises in relationships, act and speak in love.

4. You listen well.

James writes, *"...be quick to listen..."* (James 1:19). Have you ever had an argument all ready to go, so that you were waiting for the other person to stop talking so you could set them straight? This is a violation of this Word of the Lord from James. If you are a leader who pursues peace, you will be known for being quick to *listen*, not speak.

To truly listen is to gain understanding. Solomon wrote, *"Blessed is the man who finds wisdom, those who gain understanding, for she is more profitable than silver and yields better returns than gold"* (Prov. 3:13-14). For the Israelite tribes, gaining an understanding was life-saving. My mom has a plaque on her wall that teaches us: "Never criticize a man until you've walked a mile in his moccasins." It's important that we take the time to understand others as we choose to live in peace with all men.

5. You speak thoughtfully.

James also writes that we should be *"slow to speak"* (James 1:19). This means we take into consideration the other person's condition or circumstances before we respond. It's possible to say the right thing, but to say it at the wrong time. It's also possible to say the right thing in the wrong way. If you are pursuing peace, you will be seen as one who thinks before speaking and chooses their words wisely. You

> YOU WILL BE KNOWN AS A PERSON WHOSE WORDS IMPROVE RELATIONSHIPS AND SITUATIONS, RATHER THAN A PERSON OUT TO PROVE A POINT.

will be known as a person whose words improve relationships and situations, rather than a person out to prove a point.

Words can turn a good situation into a disaster in seconds. Wisdom means not always saying every word that comes to mind. Reflect on your thoughts and edit your words. When said, they can't be easily taken back.

Don't try to put out a fire using gasoline. Sometimes the best thing to do is to stop talking.

6. You keep emotions in check.

By now you've figured out there is a James 1:19-20 theme going on in the middle of these peace-pursuing actions. If you are a leader who pursues peace, you will be *"slow to anger,"* as James says. When anger takes over the only thing we can think about is getting what we want. That is why James tells us that rarely does our anger lead to the righteousness of God. Generally, we do not make good decisions when we're angry because we usually do not care about the consequences of our decisions at that moment. I don't know about you, but the angrier I become, the more convinced I am that I can read what's going on in somebody else's mind. And I can't.

7. You live in reverse when needed.

The leaders in our Joshua story acted in reverse of James's warnings. First, they got angry. Second, they spoke vigorously out of that anger. Third, they listened. I've often been guilty of living in reverse. Too many times the first step we take is to turn up the heat and bake our attitudes and thoughts for a while. If you mess up and don't listen, speak too quickly and angrily, put it in reverse. Peace-pursuing leaders are humble enough to ask for a redo.

Putting others first and the pursuit of peace is not natural. Just look at two toddlers trying to play side by side. Parents say, "We need to share with our friends" and "We don't hit our friends" ad nauseam until kids get it.

8. You choose gentleness.

Unity is more something we maintain than something we create. We maintain unity with a spirit of gentleness, not arrogance. Galatians 6:1 says,

"Brothers...if someone is caught in a sin, you who live by the Spirit should restore that person gently...." Some versions render it: *"...in a spirit of gentleness."* Gentleness is a choice, not a feeling. Monumental leaders are not ruled by emotion, but by the Word of God. We do what's right, not what feels good.

WE MAINTAIN UNITY WITH A SPIRIT OF GENTLENESS, NOT ARROGANCE.

If you are praying for reconciliation, unity, and a sense of oneness, understand that communication must take place, and it must be done in a spirit of gentleness. If you are a person who has been wrongly accused, you would do well to remember the wise counsel of Solomon in Proverbs 15:11: *"A gentle answer turns away wrath, but a harsh word stirs up anger."*

God Is the Author of Peace

> *"Make every effort to live in peace with all men and to be holy;*
> *without holiness no one will see the Lord. See to it that no one*
> *falls short of the grace of God and that no bitter root grows up*
> *to cause trouble and defile many"* (Hebrews 12:14-15).

Joshua dedicated an entire chapter of his book to this internal conflict. Why so much detail? Because while God desires for us to live in harmony, fights, quarrels, and wars do happen. It happened then, and it happens now. We have a heavenly Father who knows His children well.

Christ, Our Peace

While dividing up the land amongst the tribes, Joshua gave certain cities to the Levites and set in motion a justice system, knowing that at times, peace would need a clear pathway. The cities of refuge were part of the design to living peacefully in the Promised Land. Of forty-eight cities allocated to the tribe of Levi, known as the Levites, six were designated as cities of refuge.

The cities were Kedesh, Shechem, Hebron, Bezer, Romath, and Golan (See Joshua 20:7-8).

These cities of refuge are a foreshadowing of Christ. Just as the cities were open to all who fled to them for safety, Christ provides safety to all who come to Him for refuge from sin and its punishment.

"We have this hope as an anchor for the soul, firm and secure. It enters the inner sanctuary behind the curtain, where our forerunner, Jesus, has entered on our behalf. He has become a high priest forever, in the order of Melchizedek" (Hebrews 6:19-20).

When I take communion, a weekly observance of eating the bread and drinking the cup, I am reminded I am deeply and personally loved by God. And without the sacrifice of Jesus, I could not be in God's presence or experience His peace. Afterward, I try to remind myself that He loves *every* person in that same way. This puts me on the same level with everyone else, even those with whom I might be struggling. Regardless of what I think about someone, Christ died for him or her. The reason God didn't tell us to like everybody is because He knows we won't or maybe that we couldn't. We won't like everyone. Instead, God tells us *to love* everyone, and that includes our enemies as well as family or friends, with whom we are at odds.

REGARDLESS OF WHAT I THINK ABOUT SOMEONE, CHRIST DIED FOR HIM OR HER.

An Object of War Becomes a Symbol of Peace

This monument is different than the others. While the other monuments were *for* the Israelites, this one is *between* them. This altar would remind future generations that they were one nation. This is similar to the United States' Pledge of Allegiance, in which we are "One nation under God, indivisible, with liberty and justice for all." This altar was their pledge to be one nation under the Lord.

When all is said and done, the sixth monument isn't torn down, but given an official name: *"A Witness Between Us — that the Lord is God"* (Josh. 22:34, emphasis mine). This altar which almost caused an epic battle became a symbol of peace for the nation. That's the kind of peace, unity, and reconciliation that comes from truth and grace in relationships.

I can think of no better time than the present to get good at the skill of pursuing peace. We live in a defensive and aggressive culture. We seem to have lost our ability to dialogue when we disagree on important issues. People seem more easily offended than ever before, and there is much we can disagree on these days. Some situations and circumstances lead us to make conclusions about an individual or group of people that are incorrect. Everything from how someone spends their money to how a person votes can cause us to jump to conclusions. We have lost the ability to talk to others without making it personal, without taking offense.

> THE ABILITY TO LAUGH IS DIVINE. DON'T LAUGH AT PEOPLE. LAUGH AT YOURSELF AND WITH PEOPLE.

The call to pursue peace can indeed be intimidating and difficult, so hold onto your sense of humor. The ability to laugh is divine. Don't laugh at people. Laugh at yourself and with people. Give God space to work in your life and in the life of those with whom you have conflict.

Give it time. Peace isn't cooked in a microwave and can't be ordered at a drive-through window. God hasn't asked us to change anybody, but He has asked us to love everybody. And since I don't have to change anyone, I'm better able to live out God's prescription for peace that Paul wrote down for us:

> *"Do not let any unwholesome talk come out of your mouths, but only what is helpful for building others up according to their needs, that it may benefit those who listen. And do not grieve the Holy Spirit of God, with whom you were sealed for the day of redemption. Get rid of all bitterness, rage and anger, brawling and slander, along with every form of malice. Be kind and compassionate to*

one another, forgiving each other, just as in Christ God forgave you" (Ephesians 4:29-32).

God doesn't ask us to do things that we're incapable of doing. That would be cruel. When we don't pursue peace, it's not for lack of ability; it's because we don't want to do it. Simply said, we choose not to pursue peace. However, we can choose to pursue peace instead because God says we can. Let's at least be as patient with others as God has been with us. And this brings us to back where we began in Romans 12:18: *"If it is possible, as far as it depends on you, live at peace with everyone."*

Beliefs >> Thoughts >> Actions >> Habits >> Character >> Destiny

Do you believe others were created by God?

Do you recognize that people are not our enemies?

If so, how do your thoughts, actions, and habits show evidence of that belief?

Carefully assess the fruit of the Spirit in your life.

How has the discipline of prayer shaped your walk with God and others?

When making plans, do you communicate them well?

Journal about what you have learned from investing in relationships.

Are you gentle with others? How does this affect your leadership abilities?

Chapter 9

MONUMENT SEVEN:
CHOOSE TODAY!

"Fight the good fight of the faith. Take hold of the eternal life to which you were called when you made your good confession in the presence of many witnesses."

—1 Timothy 6:12

Transitions

DURING THE SUMMER following my graduation from Central High School in San Angelo, Texas, I worked two jobs. One was at a landscaping company and another was at a cash-and-carry office supply store. These jobs were stepping stones to my next job. I was saving enough money to pay for my trip to Phoenix to work at Unidynamics where my grandmother was an inspector.

When the time came for me to leave Texas for Arizona, I packed up my 1971 AMC Ambassador and hooked my Honda CB175 motorcycle to the back. As I stood by the car ready to leave, Dad came out and wanted to talk. He said, "I want you to know that I'm proud of you and I wish I had an inheritance to give you, but I don't. What I do have to give you," he continued, "is my name. I have worked to keep my name good. You can go anywhere in the world and use my name, and you will never be embarrassed or find that I owe anyone anything." He hoped that I would keep my name pure so I could pass it on one day to my children. During my long drive to Phoenix I thought about the name Dad had given me, and I was thankful for it. Today, I know how valuable a good name is and what a gift Dad gave me with his send-off speech and advice on that hot Texas day in the summer of 1980.

Farewell Speeches and Final Warnings

In times of transition, like graduations, weddings, as well as when we near the end of our lives, we have a need to share a last word or nugget of wisdom. Talks like that matter, whether we are the giver or the receiver. Israel was going into a time of rest, and Joshua was nearing the end of his life. He had completed what God called him to do, and he gave a farewell speech. Transitions of leadership can be tenuous. Joshua reminds the people of what he has done and God's faithfulness. He also gives them personal warnings.

Yet again, Joshua turns to the words that have become the theme of his life: Be strong, be courageous, be obedient. From Moses's apprentice to a strategic, faithful, mighty warrior, Joshua stands at 110 years old, giving his final instructions. While the story of Israel had shifted from war to peace, Joshua was well aware of the enemies that remained, mostly within the nation itself. How would they live now that the land had been subdued? How would they navigate faith in times of peace?

Joshua's words contained a strong emphasis on obedience, knowing the nation's propensity for following foreigners and getting easily distracted. He warned them of the enemy within and of becoming complacent.

"Do not associate with these nations that remain among you; do not invoke the names of their gods or swear by them...hold fast to the Lord your God, as you have until now" (Joshua 23:7-8).

Joshua knew full well that some battles weren't fought with swords and spears, hailstorms and falling walls. The battles within are fought by holding fast to the Lord. It's interesting that this monument is only one stone. That's it. Not impressive or imposing. To me it symbolizes that faith in God is decided one person at a time. This is true even for those who grew up

THE BATTLES WITHIN ARE FOUGHT BY HOLDING FAST TO THE LORD.

in a family or church where faith was prominently on display. Each member of the family must carve out his or her own faith. Each person in each generation asks, "Based on God's promises and faithfulness, will I follow Him?" Often, it is the battle that rages within us, rather than any external enemy, that keeps us from living the Promised Life. This chapter, like our mentor's final speech, is designed to help you win the battle within. It starts with God.

Re-examine Your Beliefs about God

In his charge to the nation, Joshua gave the Israelites a choice.

"But if serving the Lord seems undesirable to you, then choose for yourselves this day whom you will serve...the gods your ancestors served beyond the Euphrates, or the gods of the Amorites, in whose land you are living..." (Joshua 24:15a).

It seems odd they would be given a choice in the matter. What is Joshua really saying here? I think he is saying that you can't have it both ways. You cannot serve the one true God and something else. We all worship something. If you choose to worship God, there can be nothing else. Joshua goes on to declare the verse he is most known for:

> JESUS MADE IT CLEAR THAT WE COULD ONLY SERVE ONE MASTER AT A TIME.

"...But as for me and my household, we will serve the Lord" (Josh. 24:15b).

The Israelites had been guilty of desiring a smorgasbord spirituality. They wanted to serve God *and* other gods. They wanted to take a little bit of this and a little bit of that and make their own religion. That doesn't sound too far off from what people do today.

Jesus made it clear that we could only serve one master at a time. Even still, we can find ourselves searching for a more desirable master, one who fits what we want and one who will conform to our beliefs about God and to our wants and desires. Jesus taught, *"No one can serve two masters. Either you will hate the one and love the other, or you will be devoted to the one and despise the other. You cannot serve both God and money"* (Matt. 6:24).

The truth is that acceptable worship in any age is based on a proper belief about God, which is why it is necessary to reexamine our beliefs about Him. Today we face the challenge of figuring out how to interact with other faiths without compromising our own. The world is not neatly divided into monolithic cultures. In many parts of the world there was a time when a person could live and die without encountering other religions regularly.

Now facing different cultural and religious practices daily is the norm for people all over the world. We are tempted to idolize political correctness and a "feel good" faith over the truth of who God is and His gospel. These are not fighting words. I believe anyone who says they believe something, but is unwilling to stand up for that belief, even

> THE TRUTH IS THAT ACCEPTABLE WORSHIP IN ANY AGE IS BASED ON A PROPER BELIEF ABOUT GOD, WHICH IS WHY IT IS NECESSARY TO REEXAMINE OUR BELIEFS ABOUT HIM.

when it brings discomfort, has a shallow belief. Perhaps they really don't believe at all. We have become soft and afraid in our culture. We fear others will be angry with our beliefs and that shocks us. We should stop being shocked that we will be persecuted for our beliefs. We should expect it as Scripture says and choose to live for God alone, like Joshua did.

The Power of Choice

Consider Dr. Victor Frankl. He was a destitute, helpless pawn in the hands of brutal, prejudiced and sadistic men during the Nazi regime. In their eyes, he was nothing, so they took everything from him. He had nothing, not even a wedding band, a stitch of clothing, or a hair on his head. He did not have freedom or family. Everything had been taken away from him. This is not an exaggeration. I share this to force a comparison between your circumstances and his. What value is it for me to find someone who is worse off than me? Does that help me?

I tell you about Dr. Frankl because I want you to gain something from him that no one can take from you. While he was in that heartbreaking and pitiful situation in which everything seemed to be stripped from him, he still had something that could never be taken. It was only one thing, but it was a big thing. He realized that he had the power to choose his own attitude.

In his book, *Man's Search for Meaning*, Dr. Frankl wrote, "When we are no longer able to change a situation, we are challenged to change ourselves."[19]

> HE REALIZED THAT
> HE HAD THE POWER
> TO CHOOSE HIS OWN
> ATTITUDE.

No matter what anyone would ever do to him, regardless of what the future held for him, the choice of his attitude was his to make. Is there anything greater than the realization that under such a great persecution as Dr. Frankl endured, one still has the power to choose? Even greater is the realization that in the normal course of life, one has that power residing within himself or herself, if only it could be called forth. Will I choose to forgive or become bitter? Will I choose to hope or give up? Will I choose to focus on God or wallow in the paralysis of self-pity? The point is that he got to choose and so do we.

Choose Today

It's easy to miss this: Joshua called the Israelites to make their choice that day. When is the best time to begin a new thing that you know is the right thing? The answer is: today! In the promised life, *now* is the time to make whatever decisions or changes that need to be made. Every time we choose to combine what we know, with faith and action, good stuff happens. God takes over. Having the mindset that you will act today, or now, on things you know to be right and pleasing to God means that no opportunity is wasted. Commit to the task that's in front of you. Don't try to solve tomorrow's problems today. Use today's actions to make tomorrow easier.

Whatever God says has permanent validity. God's Word is relevant, time-less, and new. His message is clear, firm, and sure. Whenever we obey it, the door is opened to health and happiness. Why wouldn't we act on what we know today? Make the call. The New Testament writer, in making applica-tion of the story of Joshua to Christians, wrote: *"For we also have had the good news preached to us, just as they did; but the mes-sage they heard was of no value to them, because they did not share the faith of those who obeyed"* (Heb. 4:2). This verse references the Israelites who had been delivered from Egypt. They heard the good news but it was of no value to them because they did not combine that news with faith. By putting into practice what you know to be true, you will find fulfillment and satisfaction...today. On the other hand, *"...without faith it is impossible to please God..."* (Heb. 11:6). The problem in our lives is not what God has said, but that we don't believe what God has said. Even so, what God says has permanent validity. When we learn to stop waiting, we begin to experience peace, con-tentment, and security in the Lord, now. God's voice is relevant today.

> HAVING THE MINDSET THAT YOU WILL ACT TODAY, OR NOW, ON THINGS YOU KNOW TO BE RIGHT AND PLEASING TO GOD MEANS THAT NO OPPORTUNITY IS WASTED.

Choose to Hold Fast

I like Joshua's words: *"hold fast..."* (Josh. 23:8) *"But you are to hold fast to the LORD your God, as you have until now."* You can only hold so many things in your hand at any given time, right? And if you think you have a hold of something good, you shouldn't let go. The Israelites were in a time when they knew God, they knew the Lord, so Joshua says to them, "Don't let go!"

You, too, have probably got a hold of something good. While there are a lot of things that can vie for your attention and things you may want to take hold of, what are the best things to grasp? What should you hold fast? God has placed the ability to hold fast to Him in every one of us. He has given us the ability to be strong, courageous, and obedient.

Our motivation to hold fast to the Lord is because...

...He is the answer.

...He fulfills His every promise.

...He is with us.

...He gives us rest.

...He gives success.

I'm okay with Him being in charge. There are times I struggle to trust and I take charge instead. Or I am tempted by something else and enticed to let go and grab hold of something different. You've probably heard the song "Jesus, Take the Wheel" by Carrie Underwood. Well, my song would be "Jesus, take the wheel back...I'm sorry I took it from You..." Sometimes holding fast to the Lord means the courage to let go of our sense of control.

> GOD HAS PLACED THE ABILITY TO HOLD FAST TO HIM IN EVERY ONE OF US.

- How are you holding fast to the Lord?
- Are you tying any of your thoughts to the past?

And while we are talking about holding fast to the Lord, I want to caution you about one thing you should not hold fast — the past.

Choose to Review the Past. Don't Live in It.

Beware of tying your thoughts to your past failures...or successes. Those thoughts will continually pull you backward and prevent healthy forward movement. They are like a cowboy who tries to ride off on his trusty horse, but forgets to untie his horse's reins from the post. Although he may mount up and desire to ride off, he won't be able to. The same is true of our personal past. Sometimes we are afraid to live without the thoughts of the past that we have, asking ourselves, "What will I do if I don't feel bad about yesterday?" "Who am I without the success of yesterday?" We fear untied from past failures and successes alike. A little beyond that fear is freedom.

Why would you review the past? Why does God review the past? I believe it was for three reasons.

First, the past can humble us. These Israelites are not in the Promised Land because of their own doing. They are standing on the faithfulness of ancestors and leaders who went before them. They are there because of God's divine intervention! *"So I gave you a land on which you did not toil and cities you did not build; and you live in them and eat from vineyards and olive groves that you did not plant"* (Josh. 24:13).

Second, reviewing the past can bring a sense of gratitude. They are no longer slaves. They are no longer wandering. They can build houses instead of pitching tents. They are home.

Third, history always has something to teach us. Reviewing the past gave the Israelites warnings for the future. They were at a crossroads. Would they take this newfound wealth and freedom for granted? Would they forget God's promises and His faithfulness to them? Would they be faithful to Him or behave like their ancestors? What about your past failures and successes? Now is the perfect time to look back and learn. God reviewed Israel's past because they were ready to move forward. Take some time to get alone with God and review your past and ask Him to use it to launch you forward! Learn from the past, live in the present, and lean into the future. Untie and ride forward because God is with you.

Choose to Point to God

Monumental leaders always point to God, not to themselves. While

> LEARN FROM THE PAST, LIVE IN THE PRESENT, AND LEAN INTO THE FUTURE.

Joshua has been a strong leader, worthy of accolades and praise, he does not get caught up in that. Even as Joshua personally warned them to be faithful, he pointed to God's faithfulness.

> "...You know with all your heart and soul that not one of all the good promises the Lord your God gave you has failed. Every promise has been fulfilled; not one has failed" (Joshua 23:14).

He knows his strength as a leader has only and always come from the Lord. I think Joshua is one of the humblest leaders highlighted in God's Word. He was always pointing to God. Maybe that was why he was found worthy to build seven monuments.

In chapter twenty-four, verse fifteen, Joshua said to those who followed him: *"As for me and my family, we will worship the Lord"* makes for a nice quote and is often found on a lot of Christian artwork that we can hang in our homes. Is it more than a platitude in your home? Joshua was committed to the Lord regardless of the decisions of others. Joshua assured the leaders that he was not calling them to do something that he was unwilling to do. He would serve the Lord, and he would lead his family to do the same.

As you motivate the people you lead, how are you pointing them to God? Where does He show up in your talks, team meetings, messages, and everyday conversations with people? After the review, which pointed people's attention to God, Joshua made a direct appeal to the people.

Choose to Throw Away Your Idols

"Now fear the Lord and serve him with all faithfulness..."
(Joshua 24:14a).

To fear God means that we hold Him in reverence and awe and tremble at His displeasure. The focus of the verb here is upon placing the Lord above all other gods. It means to honor Him and Him alone. What does faithfulness look like for these Israelites? Joshua was very clear. It looked like throwing away any other gods. Joshua spoke bluntly about this. It could have been easily missed in all the excitement of living free in the Promised Land. His command referred to the literal, physical removal of these gods and idols from their homes and their land. Idol worship had been a hallmark, not only of Israel's distant ancestors or of their more immediate ancestors in Egypt, but even of themselves in the land of Canaan. Joshua's charge was that the nation had never truly rid itself of false worship, and he was urging the people in the strongest terms possible to do so now. He continues: *"Throw away the gods your ancestors worshiped beyond the Euphrates River and in Egypt, and serve the Lord"* (Josh. 24:14b).

Most of us are not inclined to bow down before images carved from wood or stone, but does that mean idolatry is dead? Of course not. Idols are still a threat. Idols are sneakier and harder to detect today. While idols have changed in form over the years, they still originate from man's worship of self—whether it is by having a particular thing in our home or by believing what is most comfortable.

In many ways, our situation is like that of the people in Joshua.

Today our idols might be called "Approval of Others" or "Tolerance and Political Correctness" or "My Denomination" or "Perfection" or "Love of Money." Yes, greed is a form of idolatry (See Colossians 3:5. Anything which competes with God for our allegiance and our service is an idol and must be renounced. Ultimately the difference between an idol and non-idol at its extreme points is:

- God-worship versus self-worship
- Serving God versus serving self

As I coach leaders, like others, we are tempted with materialism, pride, and ego. These sometimes creep in as idols. The fulfillment of self to the exclusion of all others is a form of idolatry. This can manifest itself in self-indulgence through destructive habits such as alcohol, drugs, and pornography, and a number of other habits, such as food, shopping, or sports, just to name a few. In the latter case, we take something intended as a blessing and turn it into an idol.

Isaiah would later write, *"Their land is full of idols; they bow down to the work of their hands, to what their fingers have made"* (Isa. 2:8). No wonder Joshua called the people to examine their belief about God. Notice this decision is made one person, one family at a time. This isn't a group decision. [20] Each person must decide what he or she believes and why he or she believes it.

Choose to Keep Your Motives in Check

Every follower of Christ, especially leaders, should look deeply inward towards the motives of their obedience. Is it out of our love for Christ and the new identity He has given us that we obey? I call this examining below the waterline. If you look at a bridge, you might see a structurally sound way to cross a ravine, a river, or the ocean. But to really gauge the safety of a bridge, scuba divers go under it to check the things we can't see. They go below the waterline. In case you are wondering, 64,000 bridges across the U.S. are considered "structurally deficient!"[21] Saul, before his encounter with Christ, was structurally deficient. He believed his obedience to the Law honored God. When he encountered Christ however, the Holy Spirit impressed on him his need to look below the waterline.

> EVERY FOLLOWER OF CHRIST, ESPECIALLY LEADERS, SHOULD LOOK DEEPLY INWARD TOWARDS THE MOTIVES OF THEIR OBEDIENCE.

Speaking about himself, Paul wrote: *"as for legalistic righteousness, fault-less"* (Phil. 3:6). On one occasion Luke records, *"Paul looked straight at the Sanhedrin and said, 'My brothers, I have fulfilled my duty to God in all good conscience to this day'"* (Acts 23:1). The theme of maintaining a good conscience was a consistent claim made by Paul. Every external command finds its starting place in the heart.

Like Joshua we do want to live obediently to the will of God. This requires diving below the waterline to honestly review the condition of your heart, your thoughts and your integrity. Leaders, we can paint a picture-perfect bridge even as it is crumbling underneath. If we are like this within, it's scary if we do nothing about it. Throw away the idols of religious perfection and public perception. Rather than attempting to follow the shifting and often shallow opinions of others, we must determine our top priority to be to follow Christ and please God.

Choose to Follow Well

I believe that every human being is called by God. We are to follow Him in all things and at all times. Everyone who has ever heard that call and obeyed has never been the same. In the same way that Joshua called God's Old Testament people to commit themselves to following God alone, we are called today to do that as well, but too often we try to follow God the way we would follow a human leader. We have lots of people we follow throughout our lives. We follow our parents and teachers, and then we follow bosses or other authority figures. There are different ways to follow. For example:

"I will follow as long as I have equal say."

"I will follow as long as I am comfortable with how and where you lead."

"I will follow you, but please understand that I also have other priorities."

When you don't fully trust the one you are following, you follow conditionally, remain in doubt, or act in rebellion. We experience that with human leadership. It's easier to follow when you fully trust the leader, isn't it?

"Follow me!" This is Jesus's simple, yet life-changing call. How are you following Him? Do you trust the One you are following? How are you following? Can you say, "I will follow, no matter what."

Our lives are shaped by the people we follow. Those who influence us strongly also affect what we worship. Worship and following are connected.

> WE MUST REMOVE ANYTHING IN OUR LIVES THAT CHALLENGES THE AUTHORITY OF JESUS IN OUR AFFECTIONS AND DESIRES.

We must remove anything in our lives that challenges the authority of Jesus in our affections and desires. We must remove anything that speaks louder in our ears and minds than the voice of the Holy Spirit. We must place God in His proper place: First! Anything that downplays the deity of God is sinful and idolatry. Ask yourself, "Is there anything in my life that keeps me from worshiping and following the one true God wholeheartedly?"

Following Jesus requires a decision. It is not a matter of mere words or superstition, as some believe. Following Jesus is a choice that is reflected in our actions.

Choose, Even When it Goes Against Everything You've Always Believed

What can happen when we throw away our idols? History shows us there can be great blessing in choosing to worship God and only God. Consider Rahab, whom we met briefly towards the beginning of Joshua. She was a prostitute and a Canaanite woman who renounced her false gods and chose the one true God saying, *"...for the Lord your God is God in heaven above and on the earth below"* (Josh. 2:11). Rahab is also commended for her faith by the writer of Hebrews: *"By faith the prostitute Rahab, because she welcomed the spies, was not killed with those who were disobedient"* (Heb. 11:31).

Rahab isn't the only example. One generation later, another woman named Ruth, a Moabite, left her culture of idol worship to follow the Lord along with her mother-in-law, saying "your God will be my God." There is an interesting connection between these two faithful women. Rahab married Salmon, an Israelite man from the tribe of Judah. They had a son named Boaz. Boaz met and married Ruth. Both women are mentioned in the genealogy of Jesus Christ in Matthew by name, a significant departure from cultural norms, in which women were never mentioned.

> *"Salmon the father of Boaz, whose mother was Rahab, Boaz the father of Obed, whose mother was Ruth..."* (Matthew 1:5).

Let this be a lesson to us all of the blessings God has in store when we throw away our idols and grab hold of the one true God.

As we are about to find out, God is holy, jealous, and the only true God.

Choose to Call Out Superficiality

The people quickly responded to Joshua's charge—too quickly. They answered Joshua saying: *"Far be it from us to forsake the Lord to serve other gods!...We too will serve the Lord, because he is our God"* (Josh. 24:16,18b). Hurray for God's people. Right? Actually, no. Joshua must have sensed their superficiality because he bluntly challenged their profession by saying,

> *"You are not able to serve the Lord. He is a holy God; he is a jealous God. He will not forgive your rebellion and your sins. If you forsake the Lord and serve foreign gods, he will turn and bring disaster on you and make an end of you, after he has been good to you"* (Joshua 24:19-20).

It might seem that Joshua should have appreciated and accepted their affirmation, but he didn't. Apparently, Joshua sniffed out overconfidence; therefore, he reminded the people the Lord is holy and will tolerate no rivals. For their own good he carefully and clearly reminded them that God is holy. He is not sinful. He is the Creator and not the creation. He is God and not man. Sometimes people say the right thing and commit themselves to something, believing in that moment they truly believe it and intend to follow through with their pledge. I have, at times, been guilty of believing what I hoped to hear from others, rather than digging into their motivation. But not Joshua. And neither should we. We need to look beyond the words coming from our mouths and examine the true motivation stirring in our hearts.

He also reminds the Israelites that God is jealous for them. He is not okay with His people worshipping other gods. And He is not okay with His people being only partially committed to Him. I think it's both funny and sad when we act offended that God is jealous for our affection and worship. Yet when it comes to our human relationships, for example, our wife or husband, we are unwilling to share their affection with another. Just as we should have healthy boundaries in our relationships with one another, God has healthy boundaries too. Because He is God, He gets to make an exclusive claim on His people. God requires absolute obedience. Does He give us room for failure? Yes. Does He accept it when we decide that it's okay to pay Him lip service? Nope. Not at all.

> MONUMENTAL LEADERS PRESS BEYOND A SHALLOW RESPONSE TOWARDS A SERIOUS COMMITMENT.

Monumental leaders press beyond a shallow response towards a serious commitment. Life is a series of choices, some small and some large. What will I eat for breakfast today? What shoes shall I wear? Whom will I marry? Which job offer should I accept? Joshua didn't let the people answer the question of whom to worship and serve like they were ordering breakfast. He made it clear this was a life-changing, life-altering decision. The people responded they would serve the Lord only.

Can I Get a Witness?

Joshua continued to press forward with the people, renewing their covenant, saying:

> *"'See!' he said to all the people. 'This stone will be a witness against us. It has heard all the words the Lord has said to us. It will be a witness against you if you are untrue to your God'"* (Joshua 24:27).

Joshua moved from "choose today..." to "this rock has heard everything you said." Joshua knew the people whom he loved and led. Like all human beings, he knew they had a tendency toward half-hearted commitment and giving lip service instead of speaking from the depth of their soul. Yet he also understood the power of choosing just as Moses had. Notice that he did not threaten, intimidate, bully, entice, sweet talk, flatter, or cajole them. He encouraged them to make an informed choice. He asked them to choose whom they would serve. "Make your choice...today," he said.

Here was a flickering flame of dedication, yet Joshua threw water on it. How quick we are to speak. But are they empty words that slide off our tongue? Or are our words spoken from the depths of our soul? In business contracts, we give our word. In marriage, we give our word, denoting our deepest commitment; we even have witnesses to our covenant. In money matters, we give our word. But most of all, and first of all, we must give our word to God, and forsaking all others we promise to worship Him alone, always and everywhere. And we must be true to that word most of all.

Choose Where You Want to End Up

How will your story end? To get more personal, do you know where you want to be when you die? I think that from the day Moses commissioned

Joshua, and quite possibly before that, Joshua lived to die in the Promised Land. Joshua began and stayed the course with his end in mind. He believed God would be faithful to His promises. Joshua lived with a sense of destiny most of us can't fully grasp. But, let's give it a try.

To understand Joshua's sense of destiny, let's look closely at his family tree. Joshua was the son of Nun, from the tribe of Ephraim. The tribe of Ephraim was direct descendants of Joseph. Joshua had no doubt heard stories of Joseph, the great Israelite who served as second in command to Pharaoh and saved his father and brothers from famine by bringing them to live in Egypt. This would have been part of Israelite History 101, especially for a young boy in the line of Ephraim, from the very house of Joseph. Earlier in the book of Joshua, two whole chapters (See Joshua 16 and 17) are devoted to the lands given to the "house of Joseph." The only other tribe to get as much attention and priority as Ephraim and Manasseh is Judah.

We also know Joshua was familiar with Joseph's legacy because he carried Joseph's dead body around, all the way from Egypt. Talk about the ultimate *Weekend at Bernie's* in real life. You and I might not understand the significance of carrying Joseph's bones around the desert, through rivers, and carting them around as you fight seven years of war, unless we consider the bigger picture.

The last chapter of Genesis is a detailed account of the end of both Jacob's and Joseph's lives. Jacob was the Patriarch to all these tribes entering the Promised Land. When Jacob died, there was a funeral procession like you've never seen. Joseph, his brothers, and all their family members, along with Pharaoh's officials and dignitaries, chariots and horsemen, made their way to Canaan near the Jordan River to a cave to bury Jacob. Only their flocks and herds were left back in Egypt. This would have been one of the stories of the "good old days" that Joshua would've heard around the campfire growing up. It must have seemed unimaginable that the Israelites, now enslaved in hard labor, were once treated like royalty in Pharaoh's palace.

After burying Jacob, Joseph and the family all returned to Egypt as they had promised Pharaoh they would. Fast forward a couple of paragraphs, and now at 110 years old, Joseph had lived long enough to see his children, grandchildren and even great, great grandchildren. Genesis says he saw the third generation of Ephraim's children. On his deathbed, Joseph made his brothers and sons promise to bury him back in the land of his forefathers. He said, *"God will surely come to your aid, and then you must carry my bones up from this place"* (Gen. 50:25). Joseph was embalmed and placed in a coffin, but never buried.

Today when someone is buried we say they have been laid to rest. Maybe, for Joseph, rest could not come until his people were at rest in Canaan. Even as his death was near, Joseph envisioned a future when God would faithfully deliver His people and restore them to the land He had promised: Canaan. We learn from Hebrews 11:22

> LIVING A PROMISED LIFE AND BEING A MONUMENTAL LEADER REQUIRES KNOWING WHERE YOU WOULD LIKE TO BE IN THE END.

that *"By faith Joseph, when his end was near, spoke about the exodus of the Israelites from Egypt and gave instructions concerning the burial of his bones."* Joseph's great, great, great, great grandson was Joshua, who was used by God to deliver this promise. I can just imagine a young Hoshea, hearing stories of Joseph's bones, and thinking, *Someday, I'm going to get out of this place and I'll take those old bones with me!*

Interestingly, both Joseph and Joshua lived to be 110 years. Both were shadows, or examples,[22] of Jesus Christ. And both, after living faithful to God during trying circumstances, were buried in the land of promise.

Living a promised life and being a monumental leader requires knowing where you would like to be in the end. For both Jacob and Joseph, it meant faithfulness and eventually being buried with their people in the land God promised. For Joshua, it meant being faithful through fifty years as a slave in Egypt, forty years wandering in the desert, and seven years conquering enemies. Despite all this, Joshua stayed the course, fearing God and serving Him only.

205

Choose Your Legacy

What legacy are you determined to leave? Is there a legacy of faith you have forgotten? Or perhaps there is a legacy of faith you want to build, and you know the only way to build it is to start it yourself. When Joshua made his personal declaration of faith and obedience to God, it is important to note that he said, *"As for me and my household we will serve the Lord."* Joshua showed he did not simply desire to see his family serve the Lord. He was determined to see it, and he was deliberately and decisively committing himself to doing the things necessary to achieve that end. Determination, not desire, is the key to the promised life God has for you.

A person's will is embodied in the actions of that person. I cannot give up my will—I must exercise it, putting it into action. I must *will* to obey. Leader, if God gives you a vision of truth, there is never a question of what He will do, but only of what you will do. Has the Lord set before you a big proposal or plan? Believe me, you will not simply drift towards success. The proposal is between you and God— *"confer not with flesh and blood"* about it (Gal. 1:16, KJV).

> DETERMINATION, NOT DESIRE, IS THE KEY TO THE PROMISED LIFE GOD HAS FOR YOU.

The vision to write this book about Joshua was planted in me twenty years ago. I desired to write the book. I even compiled countless notes on the subject...for twenty years. My desire had to move to determination. God finally got a hold of me in prayer.

At the start of each year, I spend time in prayer, asking God what my goals for the year should be. I like to set goals. Most leaders I know thrive when there is a goal set before them. I prayed. God answered. He said, "You have experience. I have given you experience." As I considered my New Year's resolutions, again I prayed, and again God answered, "You have one goal. You must be resolved about one thing...you must be resolved to write the book. That is all for now...until it is finished."

I knew that to move forward on this goal would stretch me and make me vulnerable. I knew finishing the book meant I had to involve other people. I had to share my notes and what I had written so far with someone other than my wife. I needed to make a greater commitment of time and even a financial investment. What you are holding in your hand is a twenty-year dream that finally got done. What dream or desire has God planted within you? Are you determined to make it happen? Have you set a goal with God over it? What is He saying to you about it?

Before you head off into your future, let's take a step back seven years to something that happened to Joshua before the first battle was fought. My hope is that this will encourage you to live your very best.

Choose to Live in Reality, not Fiction

An example of God's presence with Joshua occurs soon after Israel entered Canaan. Israel was camped at Gilgal, and Joshua was out taking a walk, probably checking out his strategy for the upcoming battle with Jericho. When Joshua was near Jericho, he looked up and saw a man standing in front of him. It happened suddenly. From where had he come? One minute he wasn't there and in the next he was. In that moment Joshua experienced a change in perspective, so that he could now see the man. The man had a drawn sword in his hand, which meant that he was prepared for battle. It was threatening. Before we get to his question, let's pause for a minute as Joshua is caught off guard by the sight of this man.

Sometimes what we need more than anything else is a renewed perspective that allows us to see reality. As I coach leaders, I often remind them that every day is a battle for perspective. There's God's perspective and then there's mine. As a leader, I want to see what God sees. There's God's truth and mine. We need His. Joshua saw something new in front of him.

Something powerful happens in the human spirit whenever we focus our attention on something outside ourselves and beyond our trouble. Whenever

I focus my attention on Christ and the eternal life that is beyond this life, I find exceptional joy and abiding peace. When I focus on joy, I am better able to break through obstacles that life presents. Not always without pain and not always on the first try. But that's life. We can learn to concentrate on what God says, rather than circumstances. I wonder how much God wants His kids to look up from their myopic, small, navel-gazing concerns to see Him, standing and ready to fight. I pray that my kids will always search for what is true and live in what's real. We don't just need a different perspective from the one we already have, we need one that sees what is in front of us, one that sees what is holy and true. A perspective that can only be seen by faith and beyond the minutia of the moment.

> SOMETHING POWERFUL HAPPENS IN THE HUMAN SPIRIT WHENEVER WE FOCUS OUR ATTENTION ON SOMETHING OUTSIDE OURSELVES AND BEYOND OUR TROUBLE.

Joshua questioned the man about his loyalties and allegiance because he did not recognize him as a heaven-sent messenger. Joshua asked, *"Are you for us or for our enemies?"* (Josh. 5:13).

Here was the man's reply and Joshua's response:

"Neither," he replied, "but as commander of the army of the Lord I have now come."

Then Joshua fell facedown to the ground in reverence, and asked him, "What message does my Lord have for his servant?"

The commander of the Lord's army replied, "Take off your sandals, for the place where you are standing is holy."

And Joshua did so (Joshua 5:14-15).

What a scene that must have been. The commander of Israel's army is meeting the Commander of the Lord's army. I don't want you to miss the Commander's response to Joshua because it has some solid application for us. Joshua wanted to know whose side He was on. Simple. This is not an unreasonable question between two warrior leaders. "Are you on our side or theirs?" What does that answer "Neither" mean? How can someone, especially a warrior, be on neither side in a battle?

God does not show up to gather opinions; He doesn't come to choose a side. He comes to take over. We are not to ask if God is on our side, although that seems like a common question. Rather than asking, "Is God on my side?" the more appropriate question is, "Am I on the Lord's side?" This distinction is important today as we face many battles – physical, emotional, relational, financial, cultural, and spiritual.

The Commander continued, *"...as commander of the army of the Lord I have now come."* And that was it. There isn't a clear resolution to this encounter, but the obvious implication is the Lord will fight for Joshua and Israel as long as they maintain the proper priorities, which we saw

WE ARE CALLED TO LIVE IN GOD'S PRESENCE. KEEP YOUR PRIORITIES STRAIGHT.

throughout the preceding chapters. The Lord was letting Joshua know, in no uncertain terms, that he was not fighting alone. It wasn't just that God was with him, but God was *for him* and *would fight for him.* Joshua needed to be able to recognize when he was in God's presence and that he could trust in Him. As long as Joshua maintained his priorities, God would fight for him. This principle still stands today: God wants our undivided loyalty and holiness in our lives.

We are called to live in God's presence. Keep your priorities straight. God had already promised Joshua that He would be with him just as He was with Moses (See Joshua 1:5), so Joshua didn't need to worry about that. I don't know about you, but I tend to live better when I am cognizant of

God's presence. The word "holy" is used for the first time in the story here in Joshua 5:15. It's a reminder for Joshua of the seventy-second talk he had with God earlier. It was a reminder that spiritual concerns, and not military preparations, were of first importance to the Israelites in their mission. Each of the monumental lessons covered in this book tie back to that initial seventy-second conversation. The principle of holiness is still relevant today. The concept of holiness: living for God because He is with us, is God's expectation from the beginning of time. The passage in Leviticus 19:2, which says, *"Be holy because I, the Lord your God, am holy"* is quoted by Peter in 1 Peter 1:16 and is still valid. God is with you right now. God's presence calls for holiness and undivided hearts, but the temptation is to see how far we can walk from God and still be okay.

> THE CONCEPT OF HOLINESS: LIVING FOR GOD BECAUSE HE IS WITH US, IS GOD'S EXPECTATION FROM THE BEGINNING OF TIME.

Why would we not rather see how *near* we could live to Him?

We Have Response-Ability

God has given humans response-ability. It's part of our original software design. Regardless what our circumstances may be, how other people may treat us, or what difficulties we face in life, it is fully within our own power to determine what kind of attitude we're going to have. The moment we turn our eyes to God, we realize He is bigger than any circumstance. Why should we spend time and energy worrying and fretting over the future or even over current circumstances? Joshua was reminding the people of their

> REGARDLESS WHAT OUR CIRCUMSTANCES MAY BE, HOW OTHER PEOPLE MAY TREAT US, OR WHAT DIFFICULTIES WE FACE IN LIFE, IT IS FULLY WITHIN OUR OWN POWER TO DETERMINE WHAT KIND OF ATTITUDE WE'RE GOING TO HAVE.

ability to choose: to worship God or worship self. This is the beginning point for all other choices.

God has been good to us, just as He was to Israel, and the proper response to God's grace is to serve Him only, always, everywhere, and in everything.

We see this power of choice all over God's story to us. We see it in Joseph while in prison, Daniel while hanging out in Babylon as a prisoner of war and in a lion's den. John chose to worship on the island of Patmos, Stephen hoped in God while being stoned and Paul, while in chains, wrote,

> *"Now I want you to know, brothers and sisters, that what has happened to me has actually served to advance the gospel. As a result, it has become clear throughout the whole palace guard and to everyone else that I am in chains for Christ. And because of my chains, most of the brothers and sisters have become confident in the Lord and dare all the more to proclaim the gospel without fear"* (Philippians 1:12-14).

The point is that no oppression of man can hold down the praise of God, or the attitude of grace we can access in Christ. Those people I just mentioned understood one simple, but powerful, truth that many Christ-followers forget. Praising God does not depend on our circumstances being praiseworthy. It is not circumstances that are praiseworthy; it is God. Why not choose to *"give thanks in all circumstances; for this is God's will for you in Christ Jesus,"* as 1 Thessalonians 5:18 says?

It's What You Do Next That Counts!

During our journey through Joshua, I hope your faith has started shifting from something that is simply available to you, to a faith that beckons you into God's adventurous will for your life—your promised life.

God still does exactly what He promises, every time, just as He did for Joshua. I pray that hope will grow in you and surround your heart like the wall around the Castillo de San Marcos in St. Augustine, Florida. As the oldest masonry fort in the continental United States, its walls stand thirty feet tall and are fourteen feet thick. May that kind of wall keep you and make you feel so secure in God's love, His holiness, and sovereignty that you will cross over into your promised life and lead others with you.

Start today. With your mind deeply set on and believing in the Lord's promises, turn your faith in God loose in every area of your life and see what happens. Now you have been made righteous through Jesus Christ, *live* courageously, like Joshua, by your righteousness in the Lord. No matter how good or bad, easy or difficult it may be, I guarantee you will not regret following God faithfully and crossing into the promised life.

> START TODAY. WITH YOUR MIND DEEPLY SET ON AND BELIEVING IN THE LORD'S PROMISES, TURN YOUR FAITH IN GOD LOOSE IN EVERY AREA OF YOUR LIFE AND SEE WHAT HAPPENS.

Beliefs >> Thoughts >> Actions >> Habits >> Character >> Destiny

Working backwards from destiny:

What specific goal are you intentionally walking toward in your life?

Do you have a mentor who believes in you with whom you meet?

Is your time with God deep and strong? Are you hungry for Him?

What character changes must you make to accomplish your mission?

What motivates your obedience?

What vision or inspiration has God given you? Do you hear His voice clearly?

To what do you hold fast?

BIBLIOGRAPHY

1   R. L. Alden, "Monument." Geoffrey W. Bromiley, The International Standard Bible Encyclopedia, vol. 3 (Grand Rapids: William B. Eerdmans, 1988), 410.

2   "This story is in Deuteronomy 13 and 14. However, we first meet Joshua in Exodus 17 when he defeated the Amalekites."

3   "Mindset - definition of mindset in English | Oxford Dictionaries," Oxford Dictionaries | English, accessed August 18, 2017, https://en.oxforddictionaries.com/definition/mindset.

4   See Romans 12:2, 2 Corinthians 10:4; and Proverbs 4:23.

5   Joshua's list of winning battles are when the Amalekites attacked Israel (Exodus 17:8-15); the Canaanites attacked Israel (Numbers 21:1-3); Sihon attacked Israel (Numbers 21:21-30; Joshua12:2-3); Og attacked Israel (Numbers 21:31-35; Deuteronomy 3:1-6; and Joshua 12:4-5); the battle with the Midianites (Numbers 31:1-8); and then the thirty-one kings in the Promised Land, which included the Hittites, Amorites, Canaanites, Perizzites, Hivites and Jebusites (Joshua 12:7-24).

6   "Velentina's Story," e-mail to Dan Holland, March 13, 2011.

7   Francis A. Schaeffer, Joshua and the flow of biblical history, (Wheaton, IL: Crossway Books, 2004), 129.

8   See Matthew 5:17-20.

9   See Romans 3:25-26.

10 See Romans 1:16; James 1:21; 1 Corinthians 4:6; and 2 John 9.

11 See Revelation 22:18-19; Galatians 1:8-9; Jude 1:3; and 2 Peter 1:3.

12 John Clayton, "WHY I LEFT ATHEISM," Does God Exist? Why I Left Atheism, October 23, 2012, accessed April 12, 2017, http://www.doesgodexist.org/AboutClayton/PastLife.html

13 World Happiness Report," Wikipedia, April 12, 2017, accessed April 12, 2017, https://en.wikipedia.org/wiki/World_Happiness_Report.

14 Charles F. Pfeiffer, with Wycliffe Bible commentary: produced for Moody

monthly (New York: Iversen-Norman Associates, 1975).

[15] The Bible defines self-deception thus: *"Anyone who listens to the word but does not do what it says is like a man who looks at his face in a mirror and, after looking at himself, goes away and immediately forgets what he looks like"* (James 1:23-24).

[16] C. S. Lewis, *Miracles,* (New York: Macmillan, 1960),133.

[17] Mike Bianchi, "Oviedo Team Stirred by Deaths of 2 Teens," Tribunedigital-orlandosentinel, May 17, 2002, accessed August 29, 2017, http://articles.orlandosentinel.com/2002-05-17/sports/0205170336_1_oviedo-high-brittany-smith-zac.

[18] "The Ladder of Inference," Infographic, accessed March 24, 2017, https://www.mindtools.com/pages/article/ladder-inference-infographic.htm.

[19] Viktor Emil. Frankl, *Man's Search for Meaning: an Introduction to Logotherapy* (Boston: Beacon Press, 1992).

[20] In Joshua 24:2 we learned that Israel's ancestors had worshiped other gods early on, when they were still in Mesopotamia. However, Joshua states that this had also been true in Egypt (see Joshua 24:14). There are two references made to the gods the Israelites had worshiped while in Egypt mentioned in the Pentateuch. First, Leviticus 17:7 mentions that the Israelites sacrificed to goat idols, and then in Deuteronomy 32:16–17, they are charged with worshiping foreign gods. In 24:15, Joshua added a third set of gods: *"the gods of the Amorites, in whose land you are living."*

[21] "State Bridge Inspection Data, Structurally Deficient Ratings," Governing magazine: State and local government news for America's leaders, accessed May 2, 2017, http://www.governing.com/gov-data/transportation-infrastructure/bridge-data-by-state-inspections-structurally-deficient-totals.html.

[22] There were several identical characteristics between Joshua and Jesus; identical Hebrew name Yehoshua which means "Yahweh is salvation", and both were leaders of Israel. Joseph and Jesus were both raised in the

"promised land", hated by their brothers, were taken into Egypt to avoid being killed, and were arrested and falsely accused. This is by no means intended to be an exhaustive list.

IF YOU'VE BEEN BLESSED BY THIS BOOK, WILL YOU HELP ME SPREAD THE WORD?

There are several ways you can help me get the word out about the message of this book...

- Post a 5-Star review on Amazon, Goodreads and other places that come to mind.
- Write about the book on your Facebook, Twitter, Instagram, Google+, any social media sites you regularly use.
- If you blog, consider referencing the book, or publishing an excerpt from the book with a link back to my website.
- Take a photo of yourself with your copy of the book. Post it on your social media – email me a copy as well!
- Recommend the book to friends – word of mouth is still the more effective form of advertising.
- When you're in a bookstore, ask them if they carry the book. The book is available through all major distributors, so any bookstore that does not have it in stock can easily order it.
- Do you know a journalist or media personality who might be willing to interview me or write an article based on the book? If you will email or mail me your contact, I will gladly follow up.
- Purchase additional copies to give away as gifts.

You can order additional copies of the book from my website as well as in bookstores by going to www.coachdanholland.com. Special bulk quantity discounts are available.

SPEAKING SCHEDULE...

If you are part of an organization who has guest speakers, or you know of an organization who might be interested in having me speak, lead a workshop or make a presentation, please contact me at: danhollandml@gmail.com.